Totally Incorrect
Volume 2

TOTALLY

INCORRECT

VOLUME 2

*CONVERSATIONS WITH **DOUG CASEY**
AS TOLD TO **JUSTIN SPITTLER***

CASEY RESEARCH

Doug Casey is a highly respected author, publisher and professional investor.
Doug wrote the book on profiting from periods of economic turmoil: his book
Crisis Investing spent multiple weeks as #1 on the *New York Times* bestseller list
and became the best-selling financial book of 1980 with 438,640 copies sold;
surpassing big-caliber names, like *Free to Choose* by Milton Friedman, *The Real
War* by Richard Nixon, and *Cosmos* by Carl Sagan. Doug broke the record with
his next book, *Strategic Investing*, by receiving the largest advance ever paid for a
financial book at the time. Interestingly enough, Doug's book *The International
Man* was the most sold book in the history of Rhodesia. He has been a featured
guest on hundreds of radio and TV shows, including David Letterman, Merv
Griffin, Charlie Rose, Phil Donahue, Regis Philbin, Maury Povich, NBC News
and CNN; and has been the topic of numerous features in periodicals such as
Time, *Forbes*, *People*, and the *Washington Post*. Doug is the founding Chairman of
Casey Research, an investment research publisher that helps self-directed inves-
tors earn superior returns by taking advantage of market dislocations.

Justin Spittler, Research Analyst, Casey Research
Originally from Omaha, NE, Justin attended Loyola University New Orleans'
College of Business. After graduating with degrees in management and econom-
ics in 2011, Justin worked several years as a commercial real estate appraiser in
New Orleans. While serving as an appraiser, Justin joined Casey Research as a
part-time analyst and contributing writer before becoming a full-time analyst in
March 2014. Justin is currently the editor of *The Casey Daily Dispatch*.

Co-Publishers:
Go2 Print Media Group
62 Hamel Road
Hamel, MN 553402

Casey Research, LLC
55 NE 5th Avenue
Delray Beach, FL 33483

ISBN: 978-0-692-09587-4

Table of Contents

Introduction

BY JUSTIN SPITTLER

We'd been talking on the phone for months.

We'd discussed stocks, bonds, and commodities. But we'd also hit on taboo topics like gender politics and America's emerging police state.

But we still hadn't sat down for a real one-on-one up to that point. That's because Doug Casey and I are rarely at the same place at the same time.

So I was thrilled when I found out that we would both be in Colorado last September. I would be living in Denver, and Doug would be just a short drive away in Aspen.

I suggested that I pay him a visit. Doug liked the idea. So, we set a date.

After sorting out logistics, Doug told tell me an incredible story of how he once drove from Aspen to the Fairmont Hotel in Denver in one hour and forty-nine minutes.

That's almost a 200-mile drive. Most people complete this journey in around three-and-a-half hours.

That means Doug was clocking more than 100 miles per hour *on average*.

He claims it's some sort of record. And I don't doubt it. After all, most people never drive that fast on the highway… let alone on winding mountain roads.

But Doug's not like most people. He's a thrill seeker. It's in his DNA to confront danger head-on.

For instance, Doug once flew to Rhodesia, or modern-day Zimbabwe, looking for investment opportunities.

The year was 1979. Rhodesia was in the middle of a civil war. Soldiers and armored cars lined the streets. Chaos was in the air.

It was basically a post-apocalyptic hellhole. And yet, Doug boarded a plane anyway. He risked life and limb to seek out opportunity.

In other words, this story of him racing from Aspen to Denver was just another classic Doug tale. It only added to his mystique.

Now, I imagine most people get a kick out of hearing these wild tales. But I don't just find these stories entertaining. I find them inspiring.

In fact, Doug's a big reason why I sold most of my belongings, turned in my house key, and left behind sunny Florida to become a digital nomad.

That's right. I took a page from Doug's book and became an international man.

Still, I'll be the first to admit that I'm not the natural adventurer that Doug is.

So, I didn't attempt to break his land speed record. Instead, I took my time. I even pulled over a couple times to soak up the beautiful scenery.

Four hours later, I arrived in Aspen. I checked into my hotel. I grabbed a quick bite to eat. Then, I made my way over to the Little Nell Hotel. Doug was sitting in the lobby reading the newspaper.

I pulled up a seat next to him. At first, we talked "shop." We discussed the markets, the marijuana industry, and bitcoin. Familiar territory.

As time passed, I loosened up. I told Doug about my recent travels. And I asked him where he would go if he were in my shoes. Without hesitation, he said "Africa."

That's not an answer you'll hear often. This is because most people wouldn't dare go to Africa. It's too dangerous and too far off the grid.

But Doug told me that's where the opportunity is. And he's right. Africa is the final frontier.

The idea of uprooting to Africa is intimidating, even to an amateur thrill-seeker like me. So, Doug and I agreed that I should spend time in Europe or Asia before "taking the plunge."

After finishing drinks inside, we joined a few of Doug's friends out on the patio. There, we talked politics, Doug's gun collection, and what I can only describe as the glory days in Aspen.

The conversation was interesting. It was entertaining. It was even downright hilarious at times.

That's because I got to see Doug in his element. He was unapologetic. He was unfiltered.

He simply said whatever came to his mind. It didn't matter if the person sitting across the table from him disagreed wholeheartedly with him.

If you've ever heard Doug deliver a speech in person, you know what I'm talking about. It's truly a sight to see.

Unfortunately, most people haven't had this privilege.

And that's exactly why we brought back *Conversations with Casey*.

You see, Doug isn't just a world-renowned speculator and an adventurer. More importantly than either of those things, he's an original thinker.

That's a rarity. These days, most people only think what they're supposed to think. They say only what's politically correct.

That's why it's important to hear from people like Doug.

So, I hope you enjoy these conversations as much as I did. As you'll discover, there's much more in these pages than remarkable stories. There are ideas, insights, and advice that could radically change your life... just like they did for me.

Sincerely,

Justin Spittler

Doug Casey on Controversial Buzzwords

———

ORIGINALLY PUBLISHED ON JANUARY 12, 2018

Justin's note: Doug Casey isn't afraid to speak his mind… even if it means offending people. That's a rare commodity. These days, most people only think what they're supposed to think. They say only what's politically correct. It's a serious problem that's getting worse every day. So, I called Doug to discuss some of today's most controversial buzzwords…

Justin: Doug, you said something during one of our recent talks that intrigued me:

"They'll say if you use bitcoin you're a money launderer, a drug dealer, a terrorist, or a tax evader. Actually, the morality involved in all those activities is worth a separate discussion… it's perverse they're always classed together."

What did you mean by that? What's wrong with grouping these people together?

Doug: It's chimpanzee think. It's group-think memes in action. Somebody in a position of authority—or even just an actor, or a news reader, or a rapper, for that matter—says something. That transforms it into something that everybody automatically believes in, thoughtlessly.

It's like the concept of political correctness. I first heard that term on *Saturday Night Live* in the early 1980s. They said "this isn't very politically correct." I thought it was part of their skit. I thought it was a joke.

Little did I know that it would become a meme. The concept didn't just catch on in society, it's come to rule it. You're supposed to be politically correct—if not, you must be a Nazi or a Klansman. Although, oddly, you might actually be a Communist or a fanatic Muslim with identical beliefs—and that's somehow acceptable. So, the concept of PC isn't a joke anymore. It's the complete opposite of a joke. It's a threat. Calling something a name that's not just inaccurate, but maybe the opposite of what it is, is dangerous, dishonest and destructive.

A lot of words are consistently misused today. Sometimes purposefully, sometimes just stupidly. What you say reflects what you think. And what you think—or at least feel—influences what you do. I did an article a while ago <u>debunking the misuse of a dozen common words</u>[1]. People who think in slogans and catchphrases are very dangerous. They turn their feelings into group moral memes. Lowest common denominator stuff.

Justin: They aren't thinking for themselves.

Doug: Exactly. That's how lynch mobs work—"Give us Barabbas! Give us Barabbas!" People should analyze these "hot button" concepts, like the four things I mentioned—and there are lots of others—on their own merits. Otherwise you'll wind up mindlessly parroting Paul Krugman, Hillary Clinton, or Kim Kardashian.

These terms shouldn't be grouped together. "These are evil things. We shouldn't even think about them. They're not even worth talking about." Did Big Brother call them Badthink in *1984*?

Justin: But you think they're worth talking about?

Doug: Absolutely. This is what made <u>Walter Block's book *Defending the Undefendable*</u>[2] such a work of genius. Everyone should read it. It's also very funny, <u>somewhat in the tradition of George Carlin</u>[3], another genius.

So, yes. We should dissect all four terms that I mentioned.

Justin: I agree. Let's start with money launderer.

Doug: Money laundering. It's the process of making money obtained from criminal activity look like it came from a legitimate source. But it's a completely artificial crime. It's made up. It was created out of whole cloth about 40 years ago, as I recall. Like most "crimes" today, it's not wrong in itself; it's wrong because some legislators passed a law.

There's nothing wrong, in principle, with money laundering.

Perhaps you got the money illegally or immorally. And, incidentally, those are two totally different concepts, where there's only an accidental overlap. But that's a big subject for a whole new conversation.

But what's wrong with redeploying capital that already exists in a perfectly legal or moral way? I would say nothing. Money is fungible. It's not like artwork—it's

---

1. www.caseyresearch.com/doug-casey-offensive-words/
2. www.amzn.to/2otgvH2
3. www.youtube.com/watch?v=OCYc06bVo0E

not so easy to trace its provenance.

Anyway, it's said that most great fortunes started with a crime. That's certainly true for the Kennedy fortune. Joe Kennedy, founder of the clan, made most of his money bootlegging, which is the equivalent of drug dealing. He also made money with stock manipulation, which is insider trading. God knows what else he was up to. Although bootlegging and stock manipulation are not, in themselves, immoral. That said, I have no doubt many other things—like murder, assault, theft—occurred in the process.

So, he laundered money. It wasn't a crime then.

It's counterproductive to make it illegal to take these so-called ill-gotten gains, and do something correct with them. It's just another Kafka-esque crime that they can arbitrarily use to hang you. At what point does capital created illegally become clean?

Money laundering is a non-crime, and shouldn't be treated as a crime.

Justin: What about drug dealers?

Doug: Today, drug dealers are automatically seen as the worst kind of scum. Drug dealers now are always looked upon as being violent, evil, immoral, amoral, just horrible human beings. But the problem isn't so much that drugs can be abused and harm the user—that's true of alcohol, tobacco, food, sex, inactivity, and a hundred other things. The problem arises when they're made illegal. All drugs should be legal[4].

Why? Well, your body is your primary possession. If you can't control what you can put in your own body, you have no freedom at all. You're, in effect, a slave.

That's the moral argument for drugs being legal. Whether they're good, bad, or indifferent is a technical issue. But it's a question of degree, as is the case with food, sex, alcohol, tobacco, sugar, and everything else.

These can all be addictive or even dangerous if they're not used in moderation.

The "War on Drugs" is foolish and destructive on every level. It should be abolished.

Justin: You explored this idea in your latest novel, _Drug Lord_[5].

Doug: Yes. In that novel, my co-author John Hunt and I tried to reform the unjustly besmirched occupation of drug lord. Our drug lord hero, Charles Knight, is a

---

4. www.caseyresearch.com/doug-casey-the-war-on-some-drugs-2/
5. www.highgroundseries.com

thoroughly good guy. There's nothing wrong with the commodity. There's nothing wrong with purveying drugs. But, as with the other subjects we're discussing, people often have a fixed idea burned into their consciousness, and they're unwilling or unable to analyze the subject rationally.

Drug dealing, whether you're a ghetto dweller or Big Pharma, is—in itself—a non-crime.

Justin: But Doug, drug dealers murder, kidnap people, and do all sorts of horrible things. How can you say they're not criminals?

Doug: That's true. But it's not because they're drug dealers. It's because they're murderers, kidnappers, or extortionists. Those are the real crimes.

But you've got to separate these ideas. Something may look gray. But gray is a combination of black and white. It shows a lack of critical thinking when people can't separate them.

Justin: What about terrorists? Surely they're criminals, right?

Doug: There's an old saying, "I'm a freedom fighter, you're a rebel, he's a terrorist."

I'm a fan of the American Revolution, but it can be said, accurately, that the rebels were terrorists. Why? Well, they were trying to overthrow the duly constituted government of the 13 colonies. And they used violence to do it.

They destroyed private property. They harmed lots of innocent people, starting with the Boston Tea Party.

Does that make them terrorists? Well, it's partly a matter of definition. "Terrorist" is a word that's usually used improperly. It turns out there are roughly 125 definitions of the word terrorist, different official definitions, used by various government agencies at one time or another.

To me, terrorism is simply a method of warfare. It can be a tactic, like artillery barrages or cavalry charges. Or it can be a strategy, used by a much stronger—or a much weaker—opponent, generally against a civilian population.

Justin: And how would you define terrorism?

Doug: I'm glad you asked because <u>I have been trying to formulate a correct definition</u>[6].

Try this, "an act, or credible threat, of violence, for political ends. It uses psychology, more than actual physical destruction, and primarily targets civilians."

6. www.caseyresearch.com/doug-casey-offensive-words/

The problem is political conflict. War is the ultimate form of politics. I think it was Clausewitz who said war is just politics by other means. And any kind of political conflict is bad in my view. In fact, since politics is all about how some people get to dominate other people, and about who decides who gets what, I despise politics.

Terrorism isn't the problem, any more than artillery barrages are. But you can't righteously accuse the enemy of using artillery, for some reason. That's somehow OK.

Anyway, terrorism will have an increasing place in politics as there are billions more people, and they increasingly live in giant cities. From a moral point of view, collateral damage is the problem. That's when an attack affects completely innocent people.

For example, the Israelis blew up the King David Hotel in their war of independence against the British in 1946. That was widely seen as an act of terrorism. But, to my knowledge, they didn't kill any innocent civilians. They only killed British military personnel. That was an effective—and in the context moral—act of terrorism.

The bombing of cities like Hamburg and Dresden at the very end of WW2, basically civilian targets killing scores of thousands of non-combatants, was an act of state terrorism. And both ineffective and immoral.

What about U.S. Marine barracks that were blown up in Beirut in 1983? That's said to be an act of terrorism, too. Insofar as it changed the public's psychology it was extremely effective.

The question is, what were those Marines doing there in the first place? If a bunch of Lebanese soldiers were in the U.S., would Americans have the right to blow up their barracks?

Justin: What about 9/11?

Doug: That's once again a different thing. On the one hand, it was simply mass murder for political motives—which is exactly the essence of war. But these things are all painted with the same brush. The alleged perpetrators argue it was simply tit-for-tat, considering that Americans have killed scores of thousands of non-combatants in the Middle East in recent years.

I'll tackle this subject in detail when we write *Terrorist*, the fourth novel in my series. The hero in that book, Charles Knight, is a good guy who's accused of being a terrorist.

In the meantime, a terrorist is not necessarily worse than anybody else that destroys other people's property or takes other people's lives. It's an issue of circumstances. But if you call somebody a terrorist today it's the end of the discussion. The first one to make the accusation wins.

Justin: Interesting perspective. What about tax evader?

Doug: That's an easy one. Taxation is the compulsory and coercive collection of money by a group, usually a government. That leads to a broader question about who they might be, and why they have that power. A big topic in itself.

I'm opposed to it because taxation is theft.

The dictionary definition of theft is "To deprive someone of his property by force or fraud." The definition doesn't go on to say "Unless you're the government, then it's not theft anymore."

Of course, they say taxation is the "will of the people." But the government isn't "all of us." It's a discrete entity with a life of its own. It's no different than General Motors, the Rotary Club, or the Mexican Zetas cartel, for that matter.

Government's interests are different from those of the people it's supposed to represent. In fact, taxation is a form of aggression by the government against its subjects.

There's no voluntarism involved whatsoever. If you don't comply, they will imprison or even kill you. Denying revenue to the State is a highly moral act in my eyes.

Think of it this way. If a mugger comes up to you and says, "Give me your wallet," would it be moral to try to deny it to him? Of course.

What if the mugger says, "But wait. I have a sick child at home. I need your money." Would it be moral for you to deny him then? I'd still say yes.

Now, suppose he says, "I had a vote with everybody else here on the block and I'm acting for them to take your wallet away so we can share the proceeds—for very good and necessary things, I assure you."

Is it still moral for you to deny him? Yes, because it's the exact same situation.

So, the idea that tax evaders are immoral is a non-starter. It's perverse. Stupid actually.

Having said that, I pay my taxes religiously. At this stage of my life, it's not worth putting myself in a position of liability. It's foolish to argue with a heavily armed group.

Justin: Most people disagree with you on this, Doug.

Doug: Of course. But most people start hooting and panting like chimpanzees whenever a buzzword is said. My experience is that when members of the public read controversial articles, they get tunnel vision after one of their hot buttons is pushed. At that point it becomes impossible to have a conversation with them. It's a cause for pessimism about the future. Humans are advancing at warp speed in technology, but at a snail's pace in rational thought.

Here's the key: Don't impinge on other people's persons or property. Beyond that, it's mostly a matter of aesthetics. And how you perceive yourself and want others to perceive you. And what kind of people you want to associate with.

In fact, all of this boils down to just one great law: "Do as thou wilt... but be prepared to accept the consequences."

Most people would never dare discuss—forget about defend—these concepts in public. It might bring down the moral opprobrium of some people. But because people in the West no longer have their own moral compass, I guess we'll have to await judgement from Hollywood.

I believe a conversation about these things makes more sense than joining a holy mob to jump on somebody because they aren't automatically hostile to a given concept.

Justin: Unfortunately, few people seem interested in having these types of conversations. They'd rather go along with the mob. Hopefully, this interview inspires some people to start thinking for themselves again.

Anyway, that covers everything I wanted to ask you today. So, thank you for sharing your unique perspective again.

Doug: My pleasure. I just fear Socrates would fare no better in America today than he did in Greece 2,400 years ago.

Doug Casey on the Best Buying Opportunity Since 1971

ORIGINALLY PUBLISHED ON DECEMBER 15, 2017

Juotin'o notoi Commoditioo aro in tho oarly inningo of a maccivo bull market. At least, that's what Doug Casey thinks. But here's the thing… He's not just talking about gold and silver. He thinks commodities, as a group, are about to take off. Read on to see why the stage is set for a monster rally in commodities…

Justin: Doug, I hear you're excited about commodities. Why is that?

Doug: Well, let me start by saying that commodities have been in a bear market for the last 5,000 years.

The real price of commodities, whether we're talking livestock, grains, energy, or metals, has been falling since the dawn of civilization.

And that trend will continue.

Justin: How come?

Doug: Because in primitive times we only had raw sticks and stones and wild animals and plants. If you found a little piece of metallic iron from a meteorite, you were the equivalent of a caveman billionaire. If you could find the corpse of a dead deer, you could fend off starvation for another week. If you found a berry bush it was as big a deal as owning a supermarket today.

You needed commodities to live—but they were rare, and unprocessed. The whole path of civilization since the end of the last ice age 12,000 years ago has been to develop technologies to increase the amounts—and lower the costs—of commodities. Commodities are the raw materials of civilization.

But now, things like nanotechnology, space exploration, and artificial intelligence (AI) are coming onstream. They're going to make raw materials super abundant, and super cheap.

These new technologies will cause commodity prices to collapse. They're basically headed towards zero.

Justin: So, why launch a new commodity letter?

Doug: Why indeed. It's a seeming paradox. We're doing it, however, because commodities are highly cyclical. And highly volatile.

It's true that commodity prices have been falling for the last 5,000 years, and that trend will continue. But that's not relevant to what will happen over the next five years. Why not? Because most are not only selling at about the cost of production, but also at a clear cyclical low. Commodities are very cheap. In both absolute and relative terms. Plus, the possibility of various financial accidents and *force majeure* loom over the markets. Political upsets and wars typically make commodities soar. Weather conditions or disease can create shortages. These are among the macro reasons I think commodities will head higher over the next five years.

They last peaked back in 2011. Many of them are still down 50%. Could they go lower? Anything is possible, of course—we could have a credit collapse deflation, for instance. But that's unlikely with today's massively inflationary monetary policy, which puts upward pressure on all prices.

Justin: Commodities are certainly cheap. I can't argue with that... but what's to stop them from getting cheaper?

Doug: Costs of production are the limiting factor to the downside. Right now, most commodity producers are just breaking even, or losing money.

That's a problem, and can't continue for too long. After all, commodities are the building blocks of civilization. You need them to survive. And the world uses more of them every year. Partly because the world's population is still growing. But in part because thousands of new uses are found for all of them every year.

There are 92 naturally occurring elements on the periodic table. Everything in the universe is made out of them. A century ago only half of them had uses; now they all have many uses.

Interestingly, the American Chemical Society recently published a paper that said a dozen or so are in already critical shortages. It said another 30 elements or so could go into short supply by the end of the century.

Silly article, from a historical perspective; I suspect they had an English major who's a member of the Green Party write it. I disagree strongly. That's because "abundance" and "shortage" in an advanced economy are functions of economics much more than chemistry. But perception often creates reality in markets. Einstein was right when he said that, after hydrogen, the most common thing in the universe is stupidity.

But perhaps they're right. If so, it's another argument to look at commodities now.

Justin: So basically, commodity prices are too low to support production. Therefore, they must rise. Otherwise, the lights go off and nothing gets built. Is that right?

Doug: Yes.

Not only that, all these governments are printing up currency units by the bushel basket.

But almost none of that new money has ended up in commodities so far. They're basically the only asset that's still cheap.

Nobody cares about commodities now. They're not "hot." Bitcoin, tech stocks, and things of that nature are the current flavor of the day.

You can see what I mean in the charts below.

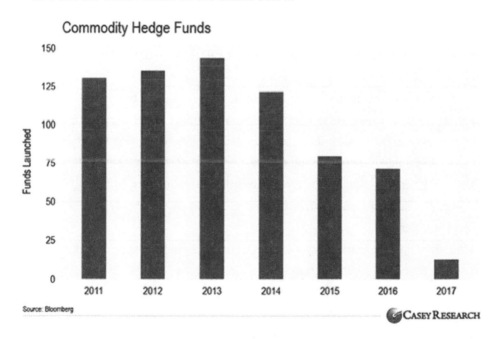

Commodity Hedge Funds

Source: Bloomberg

CASEY RESEARCH

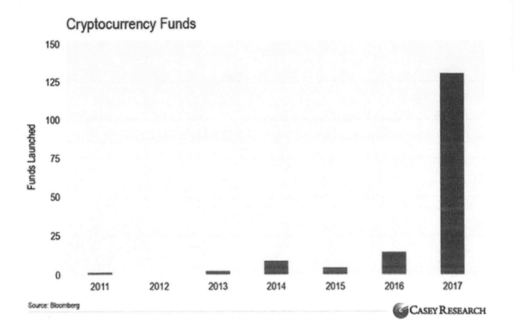

Cryptocurrency Funds

Source: Bloomberg

CASEY RESEARCH

But if you want to make money, you've got to buy straw hats in winter. You need to buy umbrellas when it's sunny, not when it's raining.

All financial markets rotate. They're all cyclical. But commodities are by far the most cyclical of all markets.

That's the basic argument for buying commodities now. In five years, I expect to be saying it's time to sell them. And, when commodity prices are at manic highs, more money can be made—and much more quickly—by going short in a bear market than by being long in a bull market.

Justin: When was the last time you saw an opportunity like this?

Doug: The last time an opportunity was this ripe was probably in 1971, before the gold standard fell.

After that, every commodity took off. Grains, livestock, energy, and the metals.

It was a monetary phenomenon then. And the same thing is happening again, albeit with a few twists. Gold, for instance, is about three times as expensive, in real terms, than it was in 1971. Say the equivalent of $120 back then. But the world's financial situation is much, much, more unstable.

I suspect one reason is because many people who normally buy gold are buying alternative assets.

Hundreds of billions of dollars have gone into cryptocurrencies alone. A lot of people who would normally buy gold are buying cryptos instead.

Justin: Are you still bullish on cryptos?

Doug: Yes, I've been bullish on them for about a year and own bitcoin, other cryptos, and shares in bitcoin mining companies.

That said—even though the trend is your friend, and they're going higher—I can no longer be wildly bullish. I mean, bitcoin's trading north of $17,000. And I like to buy things when they're demonstrably cheap. That's not true of bitcoin anymore.

Bitcoin's been in a bubble for some time now. And that bubble's probably going to get much bigger. You've got to make the trend your friend—and the trend is still up. As far as crypto fundamentals are concerned, I'll stand by what I said in these past *Conversations with Casey* (here[1] and here[2]).

I like to buy things when they're demonstrably cheap. That's not true of bitcoin anymore. But it's true of commodities now.

Just look at this chart. It tells you everything you need to know.

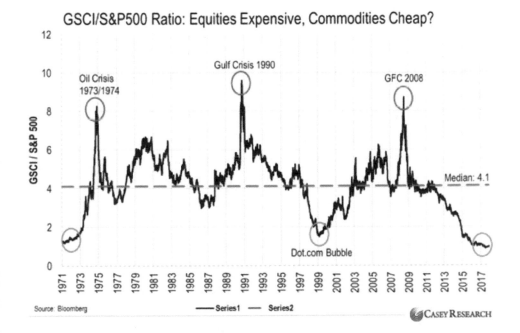

GSCI/S&P500 Ratio: Equities Expensive, Commodities Cheap?

Source: Bloomberg

Series1 — Series2

CASEY RESEARCH

---

1. www.caseyresearch.com/doug-casey-on-why-bitcoin-is-money
2. www.caseyresearch.com/doug-casey-on-why-bitcoin-could-hit-50000

Justin: So, how are you betting on commodities? Have you "backed up the truck" on junior miners?

Doug: Well, I generally do like to sell put options against very cheap commodities.

I do this because when you sell an option, it's a wasting asset. So, you win if everything just stays the same.

In other words, you don't have to be very right when you sell options. You just need to not be very wrong.

So, I'm selling out-of-the-money puts on things like wheat, soybeans, cattle, and copper.

Is it risky? Sure. That's because anything can happen. But in today's world it's one of the best risk/reward propositions out there.

If, for instance, there's a major drought in a country that produces a lot of wheat, the price of wheat can jump up 50% in a day. Incidentally, almost nobody gets it right when they're asked what country is the world's largest wheat exporter. They think it's the US, or Canada. But it's Russia. Things change.

If there's a civil war in the Congo, copper prices could move up radically. On the other hand, if the stock market crashes, so might cattle prices—because people would be less able to afford beef. There are 100 commodities that are traded, and 1,000 things that influence their prices, in both directions.

That's why I'm interested in the area. It's a key sector of human knowledge. And today, when most kids think milk comes out of a carton, not out of a cow, it's an unlevel playing field. I like it when the field is tilted in my direction...

Justin: Doug, what about the financial hurricane that hit in 2007? You've been saying that it will make landfall again for a while.

That would obviously be bad for stocks. But what about commodities?

Doug: Well, let's think about this.

Historically, there have been lots of times when commodities have done well when stocks haven't.

They're basically contra-cyclical. Right now an excellent long-term move is to short (bet against) stocks and get long (buy) commodities.

One reason for that is that high commodity prices raise production costs for companies. And when food prices rise, people have less money to spend on discretionary items. Companies earn less because of that.

Justin: So, why is almost no one else talking about this opportunity in commodities?

Doug: These days, people are used to dealing in digits on the Net, in the Ether, up in the Cloud. It's like an artificial reality. The world ceases to exist if they lose their iPhone. They only appreciate the digital world, and companies like Facebook and Amazon.

Commodities people, however, live in the physical world. They're playing in the sun with cows, dirt, oil, and big yellow machines. This is where reality exists, much more than on a plastic device.

It's gotten to the point where you almost need to be long commodities, if only as a contrarian play. And that's coming from someone who says commodity prices have been falling in real terms for the last 5,000 years.

Justin: Doug, we've spoken a lot about commodity prices and mean reversion. But what about the demand side? What's the appetite for commodities looking like?

Doug: That question requires a sophisticated answer. Three-quarters of the people on this planet are poor. And they want all the things that Americans and Europeans have.

They want to eat a lot more beef and bread. They want refrigerators, air conditioners, cars, and everything else that we take for granted. That requires a lot of raw material.

Commodity prices will go way up if we have a major war. And the clock on the wall is telling me that a major conflict is in the cards. I'm not talking about another sport war like the ones the US has been having in recent years, either. And that's bullish for commodities.

On the other hand, technology keeps getting better. Things always tend to become more efficient. I used to get 10 miles to the gallon in my car back in the old days. Now, cars get 15, 20, even 30 miles to the gallon.

Not only that, it takes far less material to make a product; manufacturing is much more efficient. Everything today is smaller and lighter. Since the 1960s, the production of everything from grains to livestock has become efficient. A typical acre yields far more grain and beef today than it did in the 1960s.

Everything's doubled or more in terms of productivity per acre.

And productivity is going to go up even more with the genetic revolution now happening. So, these things are bearish for commodities over the long run. We don't care. You can play the trends both ways.

Justin: And what force is more powerful? Is it the rising middle class in places like China and India or more efficient technology?

Doug: It's a tug of war. That creates volatility. And that, in turn, creates opportunity. Right now, it's a huge opportunity on the upside.

Justin: Exciting times, indeed. Anyway, that's all I have for you today. Thank you for sharing your insights again.

Doug: You're welcome.

Doug Casey on Why Millennials Favor Communism

———

ORIGINALLY PUBLISHED ON DECEMBER 1, 2017

Justin's note: Communism is better than capitalism. At least, that's what a growing number of young people in the U.S. think. I wish I were joking. But a recent study from the Victims of Communism Memorial Foundation, a D.C.-based nonprofit, found that half of the millennials it surveyed would rather live in a socialist or communist country than a capitalist society. And 22% of those surveyed had favorable views of Karl Marx… while 13% viewed Joseph Stalin and Kim Jong-un as "heroes." To figure out what's behind this disturbing trend, I called Doug Casey…

Justin: So Doug, about half of U.S. millennials would rather live in a socialist or communist country… What's gotten into the youth?

Doug: The youth are being corrupted, and it's more serious than ever.

I say that a bit tongue-in-cheek, however.

That's because one of the two charges against Socrates when he was executed in Ancient Greece was corrupting the youth. Older people always think the youth are foolish, ignorant, lazy, crazy, and generally taking the world to hell in a handbasket. And of course many of their charges are, and always have been, true.

But as kids get older, they generally get wiser, more knowledgeable, harder-working, and more prudent. Nothing new here. The world has survived roughly 250 new generations since civilization began in Sumer 5,000 years ago. And it will likely survive this one too.

That's the bright side. And, as you know, I always look on the bright side. But, on the other hand, the American university system has been totally captured by Cultural Marxists, socialists, statists, collectivists, promoters of identity politics, and people of that ilk. These people hate Western Civilization and its values, and are actively trying to destroy them.

Justin: How'd that happen? Don't young people go to college to learn how to think critically?

Doug: When the average 18-year-old goes to college, he knows very little about how the world works in general. He's got vague ideas he picked up mostly from TV, movies, and people who got a job teaching high school. They know roughly nothing about economics, government, or history. Worse, what they think they know is mostly wrong.

That makes them easy prey for professors with totally bent views to indoctrinate them.

It's not so much that they're taught inaccurate facts. There are plenty of "factoids" (artificial facts), of course—like the War Between the States (which shouldn't be called the Civil War) was mainly fought to free the slaves. Or that Keynesian economics is correct. And many, many more. But that's just part of the problem.

It's not the factoids they're taught. It's the way the schools interpret actual facts. The meaning they infuse into events. The way they twist the "why?" of events, and pervert concepts of good and evil.

The real problem, however, is that, contrary to what you suggested a moment ago, they're not taught critical thinking. Rather just the opposite—they're taught blind acceptance of what's currently considered politically correct.

Instead of questioning authority in a polite and rational manner—which is what Socrates did—the current idea is to prevent any divergent views from even being discussed. The profs are basically all socialists, and the kids tend to believe what they're taught. Those views are buttressed by the other sources of information available to them—Hollywood, mass media, and government.

These bad ideas usually start with "intellectuals." Intellectuals typically despise business and production, even though they envy the money the capitalists have. Intellectuals feel they're not only smarter, but much more moral. That gives them the right, in their own eyes, to dictate to everyone else. That's one reason why they're usually socialists, and approve of a "cadre," like themselves, ordering everyone else. Intellectuals naturally gravitate to the university system, where they're paid to hang out with each other, be lionized by kids, hatch goofy ideas.

This has always been the case. But it's becoming a much bigger problem than in the past.

Justin: How come?

Doug: A much, much higher percentage of kids go to college now than have ever gone to college in the past.

In the recent past, maybe five or a max of 10 percent of kids went to college. These days, almost everybody goes. So a much higher proportion of the youth are being infected with memes that the leftists have put in there.

So yeah, some kids will grow out of it, and will realize that most of what they've paid an exorbitant amount of money to learn is nonsense. But most will reflexively believe and defend what they were taught in the cocoon. And I'm afraid those people now make up a big chunk of the U.S. population.

So yeah, I think the numbers that are quoted in that article, about how many kids think socialism is good, are probably accurate. And if they don't think it, almost all of them feel it. Few know the difference between thinking and feeling...

Justin: Today's universities aren't just teaching bent ideas about politics and economics. They're also dispelling insane notions on race.

For example, an anonymous student at Tulane University in New Orleans recently posted a sign that read "It's okay to be white."

Nothing wrong with that, right? Well, apparently the Tulane administration wasn't pleased. Here's an official response from Tulane's public relations department.

We have no idea who posted these signs, but that person is obviously not speaking for Tulane University.

I got a chuckle reading that. But it's a disturbing sign of the times. Wouldn't you agree?

Doug: Yeah, it borders on the unbelievable. The insane, actually.

Most whites have been indoctrinated, both indirectly and directly, subtly and overtly, over the years. They've bought the propaganda that being white is bad. They believe Western Civilization is a bad thing... that white people have destroyed the world.

Even if they don't want to believe it, because the concept is so stupid and so utterly contrafactual, they end up believing it just because they've heard it over and over. It's very bad news across the board.

Justin: The mainstream media seems to be peddling these bad ideas, too. Wouldn't you agree?

Doug: Absolutely. The memes that originated with intellectuals in universities have thoroughly infiltrated the mass media and the entertainment industry—places "thought leaders" gravitate towards.

And you're getting no defense at all from so-called capitalists and business leaders. All they're interested in is making money. And—absolutely if they're wired with the Deep State—they don't really care how they do it. They're happy to work with and for the government. They self-righteously make charitable contributions to universities and NGOs, subsidizing the source of the poison.

So, there's almost nobody to defend the ideas that have brought us Western Civilization. And—with the exception of a few anomalies like Taoism, yoga, and Oriental cooking—it's responsible for about everything that's good in the world. Without it the whole world would resemble Africa, or Cambodia, or Mongolia—not even today, but 200 years ago. Western ideas are things like individualism, freedom of thought, freedom of speech, science, rationality and capitalism. These concepts no longer have any defenders anywhere. They're under attack everywhere.

Justin: This can't be good for the economy in the long run.

Doug: No. It's one of the reasons I'm generally bearish.

I mean, how can the markets be healthy when what's left of the ruling class in the country actually hate themselves? When the middle class is collapsing? When political entrepreneurship is valued more than making money through production?

In fact, the economy and the markets are the least of our problems. The very foundation of civilization itself is under attack. The acceptance of destructive ideas is getting to be as serious as what we saw in Russia under the Soviets, in Germany under the Nazis, or China under Mao. More serious, since civilization is under serious attack in the U.S., which has been the bulwark for the last century.

So, excuse me for my bearishness, but I think it's warranted.

Justin: Thanks as always, Doug.

Doug: You're welcome.

Doug Casey on the Paradise Papers

———

ORIGINALLY PUBLISHED ON NOVEMBER 22, 2017

Justin's note: People are outraged over the Paradise Papers. The Paradise Papers are a collection of more than 13 million confidential documents. They relate to offshore investments. Someone stole these documents from Appleby, a law firm based in Bermuda, and leaked them to the press. But that's not why people are upset. Instead, they're mad that rich people are using offshore accounts to pay less taxes. It's completely ridiculous. So, to make sense of this, I called Doug Casey…

Justin: Doug, what do you make of all this hysteria surrounding the Paradise Papers? Should the public be upset, or even surprised, that rich people are trying to reduce their tax burden?

Doug: It's a sign of the times for several reasons. And none of them are good. It's a sign of terminal moral sickness.

First, the mob is howling about the fact that rich people would dare to get their money offshore to jurisdictions where the taxes are lower. The cancer of envy is very advanced in the Western body politic. Envy is different from, and much worse than jealousy. Jealousy says: "You have something I want. If I can't get my own, maybe I'll take yours." Envy says: "The very fact you have something I want, but don't think I'll ever get, makes me hate you. I'll destroy both you and the object if I can."

Number two, it shows the average person now resents rich people for having a modicum of privacy in today's world. Privacy is a signature of civilization—there is no privacy in primitive societies, where everyone can see and hear what's going on in the next hut. Today the average guy intuits that Google, the NSA, Facebook, and a hundred other entities, including his new "smart" refrigerator, know everything about him. He resents that some people don't want to be an open book to the world, and can avoid it.

And finally, there's no outrage about the fact that these papers were stolen from a law firm. Nobody is even acknowledging that an actual crime was committed. Nobody cares about the thieves being punished. Instead, they're on an envy-driven witch hunt against the victims.

There's no outrage at all, except against the victims, which is very disturbing. It's yet another sign that one of the central values of Western civilization is going under.

Justin: I agree that there should be much more outrage over the actual crime that was committed. But doesn't the average Joe have reason to be upset by this? I mean, "the system" clearly favors the rich, right?

Doug: Of course. The system of income and asset taxes is totally corrupt. The problem isn't some people evading and avoiding tax to preserve their assets. The problem is that the *hoi polloi* want to see them pay their "fair share"—whatever that is—instead of eliminating or greatly reducing taxes. Rich people have the money to hire lawyers to make sure that laws are passed, and manipulated in their advantage. They have the money to hire accountants to take advantage of all the loopholes in the laws. They have the money and the connections to bribe politicians to make sure things are passed in their favor.

So yes, the system is very much oriented towards the rich people, and that's not good. But it wouldn't be that way if the world wasn't so politicized, where the government's not in a position to pass out favors.

In other words, the rich are getting richer, but it's largely because the government is getting bigger and more powerful, and the rich are able to take advantage of it, for the reasons I mentioned.

And to keep the pot from boiling over, they give the plebs some welfare benefits. Free this and free that. Some bread and circuses, as it were.

The whole society has become quite corrupt. It's become a giant circle jerk, where everyone is trying to live at the expense of everyone else.

So, you're right. The plebs have plenty of reason to be angry about the rich patricians. Bill Gates and Jeff Bezos alone have more assets than the lower 50% of American society put together. They deserve to be multibillionaires—they've created a lot of wealth. But they were also complicit with the government in the process, helped by public funds.

But the rich have plenty of reason to be angry, too. They're paying almost all the taxes, while the bottom 50% not only pay nothing, but are net recipients. Which is very corrupting.

This is all indicative of an underlying atmosphere of class warfare in the United States, and all over the world. It's explosive.

Justin: Doug, you said earlier that this is "a sign of the times." Does that mean that this anti-rich rhetoric will get louder?

Doug: I think so. You've got to keep in mind that since the so-called "Great Recession" started in 2007, interest rates have gone to zero in nominal terms, and less than zero in real terms.

This has made it possible for the wealthy people to borrow obscene amounts of money, and take advantage of the bubbles this money has created in the financial markets.

At the same time, these policies have encouraged poor people to buy houses, cars, trinkets from China, and so-called educations that they can't afford. Consumer goods that depreciate.

When we get out of the eye of this hurricane, and enter the storm's trailing edge, it's going to last much longer, be much worse, and be much different than the unpleasantness of 2008 and 2009.

I've said that many times before, but it bears repeating again and again. The natives are going to get quite restless, because the same thing is going to happen. They're going to lose their houses, they're going to lose their cars, they're going to lose their jobs.

This time we'll likely see high retail inflation. The high inflation is going to devastate them in any number of ways, making it even harder for them to get ahead than it is now. Times will get much worse, not just economically, but politically, and sociologically. Perhaps militarily, which is really scary. They might start a serious war. I don't know if it'll be with North Korea, or Iran, or Russia, or one of a dozen other countries.

A serious war, not a sport war, which is the kind we've had so far in Iraq and Afghanistan.

Justin: Doug, what side will the government take if class warfare escalates? Will they side with the rich or poor?

Doug: That's a good question. And the answer, I think, is that they'll take the side of the really rich and the really poor.

The really rich people have all the money and the really poor people have all the votes. Who's going to get screwed is the middle class, which is diminishing in both size and power daily.

One of the things that made the United States of America was its huge middle class. That's changed. Now, it's turning into two classes, both puppets of the Deep State: the Masters of the Universe and the *capite censi*, or head count, as the Romans called them. The natives may get very restless.

I think the government will favor the two extremes. And the middle class will get screwed further. It's going to be ground, as Lenin said, between the millstones of inflation and taxation.

Justin: What would you say to people who belong to the middle class? Is there anything those folks can do to protect themselves?

Doug: Not very many people have prepared very well for the kind of tough times that I think are coming.

They should own gold, which is very reasonably priced right now. It's not a giveaway like it was in 2001 or 1971, but it's still very reasonable. They ought to be buying gold coins.

We're entering a speculative environment for gold. A real bull market. It happens cyclically.

Remember, however, that gold mining stocks are not good businesses. They aren't long-term holdings. They're burning matches.

But they should become the object of a super bubble sometime soon. They're the most volatile securities on the planet.

Justin: Is there anything else folks can do to insulate themselves?

Doug: Well, today's problems have deep political roots. So, you have got to diversify politically if you can. But I'm afraid many people aren't in a position to do so.

However, if you have the means, you should try to diversify politically and geographically. Get outside of your home country.

It will improve your standard of living. It'll improve your prospects of doing well. It might even reactivate your psychology, which might be getting pretty beaten down at home.

Justin: What do you mean by that?

Doug: One of the most disturbing things that's come up in recent years is that white males that are middle class and below are living shorter lives. This is unprecedented, and disturbing. It's further proof that the middle class is collapsing. For a lot of people, reactivating their psychologies is as important as anything else. Most everything is a matter of either economics or psychology.

It's not "steady as you go." People are going to have to start thinking differently, and making some changes, or they're going to be blindsided. As ugly as 2008 and 2009 were, what's coming up is going to be much worse.

Justin: Thanks as always, Doug.

Doug: You're welcome.

Doug Casey on Why You Shouldn't Worry About Russia

ORIGINALLY PUBLISHED ON NOVEMBER 21, 2017

Justin's note. Russia is Public Enemy No. 1. At least, that's what the mainstream media is saying. According to most news outlets, Russia hacked Hillary's email server. It's said they rigged last year's presidential election. And now, they're supposedly using social media to divide the United States. *The New York Times* recently said these attacks represent "an unprecedented foreign intervention in American democracy." Now, that may be true. But I still can't help but wonder if the average American should be worried about Russia. So, I asked Doug Casey to weigh in on this matter...

Justin: Doug, just how big of a threat is Russia to the U.S. right now?

Doug: This is a tempest in a tiny little toilet bowl. The Russians are not a threat at all.

I've often described Russia as being nothing more than a gun store attached to a gas station in the middle of a wheat field. And that's all it is. It's not an economic power.

The country suffers from chronic alcoholism, and is in perhaps terminal demographic decline. It's not an economic power. It's not even a military power anymore. This hysteria about the Russians is crazy. It's a fabrication of what Eisenhower called the military-industrial complex. They're in back of this spate of Russophobia as well as the insane sport wars the U.S. is fighting all over the world.

Justin: So, they're not a threat to the U.S. in the traditional sense. But what about in today's digital world?

Doug: In other words, did they hack the election? That impresses me as ridiculous on its face. For all we know, if some foreign computer was addressing U.S. voting machines, maybe it was a couple of Russian teenagers playing around.

Maybe they decided to set up a Facebook presence, one being pro-Muslim, one anti-Muslim. Maybe one pro-gun, anti-gun; or pro-black, anti-black. And were just experimenting to see how it worked out. And maybe some Russian bought a few thousand dollars of political advertising as a goof. So what?

And why should this only be the Russians? People all over the world can set up Facebook presences or buy a few thousand dollars of advertising, a trivial amount. I mean, it's not even enough to be called a rounding error. Then you get some politically motivated American hysterics trying to make it into a big deal.

Even if the Russian government were directly or indirectly involved in trying to influence the U.S. elections, the answer is, "Why not?"

Justin: What do you mean?

Doug: U.S. elections influence the rest of the world. The Russians, the Europeans, Koreans, Chinese—everybody—have a huge stake in who the Kardashian-watching Walmart shoppers vote for in the quadrennial popularity contest. If the U.S. Government didn't have hundreds of military bases around the world, and didn't control the world's financial system, they wouldn't care nearly as much.

Not only that, the U.S. has a long history of actively, violently, and directly influencing the elections in foreign countries in every way possible, most recently in the Ukraine. And if that doesn't work, fomenting a coup d'etat.

Most of what's in the news, certainly its interpretation, is make-believe by who knows who. You have a talking-head newsreader, repeating what's on the teleprompter. The people who write his script haven't been on the scene either. The news is like a group of kids playing the game of telephone. But worse, because kids don't have an agenda. Most of this is hysteria fomented by denizens of the cesspool known as the Democratic Party. It's a gigantic pot calling a tiny little kettle black.

I'm much more concerned about various Americans hacking election machines. They've got a vastly more direct interest in who wins than the Russians, or any other foreigners.

Justin: So, it's obvious you're not worried about Russia. But why do you think so many other people are?

Doug: Americans—in particular elements of the U.S. Government—are just looking for a foreign enemy at this point—someone to blame for whatever problems they have. And the Never Trump people are looking for something, real or fabricated, to pin on him.

It used to be—back in the '70s—that Americans would blame the Saudis for making the price of oil too high, or maybe too low, and then they'd say, "Well, we'll just confiscate their assets here in the U.S." It's helpful to have a foreign enemy for domestic problems.

This dangerous meme started floating around in the U.S. The type of thing you'd expect only from a banana republic, where it's SOP to fabricate some excuse to nationalize—which is to say steal—foreign property. And then the Chinese became the enemy of the day, and needed to be punished for filling U.S. stores with affordable merchandise. Now the North Koreans are the enemy of the day—a complete non-entity of a little country. Certainly, no threat to the U.S.—unless you provoke them with annual military exercises and multiple carrier groups off their coast, as we do. The North Koreans may be a problem for the South Koreans, the Chinese, the Japanese, and others in the region. It's insane to make them into a U.S. problem.

Justin: Don't forget the Mexicans. Haven't you heard? They took all our manufacturing jobs.

Doug: Yeah, the Mexicans. They're an excellent excuse to "unite" Americans. The problem is that Americans barely even have a culture anymore. And, assuming being united is a good thing, which is questionable, it's now impossible anyway. We're now "multicultural"—Mexicans, Somalis, Kenyans, Iraqis, Pakistanis—people that generally don't understand what it means to be an American. Nor do they particularly care to find out. The days of *Leave It to Beaver* and *Father Knows Best* are in the distant past.

Today's Russians are actually more culturally similar to the old America than the new multicultural U.S. is.

Justin: What about the U.S. government? What if anything should they do to prevent foreign "trolls" from influencing the political discourse in this country?

Doug: The government is always looking for an excuse to "do something," and solve an imaginary problem. As I said before, I'm much more concerned about domestic than foreign enemies. For one thing, there are a lot more of them—there are more communists in the typical U.S. university than there likely are in all of Russia. And, apart from that, how are they supposed to stop foreigners from having opinions, and dispensing them to Americans? Have a news blackout from abroad in the months before every election?

In the end, it all just exposes what a charade "democracy" is in today's world. The voters in the U.S. can be swayed as easily as the mob at the funeral in Shakespeare's *Julius Caesar*, listening first to Brutus then to Marc Antony. People elect candidates based on emotional impressions, hearsay, and fake news. It's quite ridiculous, and embarrassing.

I guess they just want to make sure all the fake news is domestic in origin…

Justin: Thanks for taking the time to speak with me today, Doug.

Doug: My pleasure.

Doug Casey on Why Race Will Break the U.S. Apart

ORIGINALLY PUBLISHED ON NOVEMBER 14, 2017

Justin's note: "America is a marvelous idea, a unique idea, fantastic idea. I'm extremely pro-American. But America has ceased to exist." This is one of Doug's more memorable quotes. I'm sharing it with you because Doug said something recently that touched on this radical idea. He said the United States could break apart due to racial tensions. Most people haven't considered this possibility. After all, the U.S. is supposedly a "melting pot" where different races can coexist peacefully…

Justin: Doug, the last time we spoke, you said the United States could break apart because of racial tensions. Why do you think that?

Doug: Well, I used to know a guy by the name of Michael Hart. He would come to our Eris Society meetings in Aspen. Eris was a private annual event I ran for 30 years, for authors, scientists, and people who were well-known for something. It enabled people who might not otherwise meet to get to know each other and exchange ideas. Michael was a university prof, best known for his book *The 100: A Ranking of the Most Influential People in History.*

One year, he gave a speech about how the U.S. was going to break up into smaller countries, and part of it would be on racial lines.

I thought that unlikely at the time; it was about 1990. Now, I think Michael may have been right.

I'll explain why in a minute. But we should first discuss the origins of democracy.

Democracy originated in 6th-century BC Greece. It was a unique and workable method of governance for city-states of a few thousand people. And in the case of Athens, as many as 40,000 people.

But these people all shared a common language. They worshipped the same gods. They were the same ethnicity. They had the same customs and beliefs.

They were like an extended clan with many similarities. Differences were among individuals, not groups.

When the U.S. democracy was started, it was much like that. It was very much like a Greek city-state, an extended one. Everybody shared culture, ethnicity, language, habits, and so forth, with just minor regional differences. People saw themselves first as New Yorkers, Virginians, or whatever, just as the Greeks saw themselves first as Athenians, Thebans, Corinthians, or many scores of other polities.

As you know I don't believe in democracy, I believe in personal freedom. Democracy is workable enough in something like a cohesive city-state. But absolutely not once voters get involved in economic issues—the poor will always vote themselves a free lunch, and the rich will buy votes to give themselves more. Democracy always devolves into class warfare.

In ancient Greece, if you weren't a landowner you weren't respected. In the U.S., voting rules were determined by the States, and originally, everywhere, you had to be a landowner. That meant you had something to lose. But that's not the case anymore.

Justin: What's changed?

Doug: For one thing, anybody can vote. People who are penniless. Eighteen-year-olds who have no knowledge or experience and are fresh out of the indoctrination of high school. Lots of non-citizens, probably millions, manage to vote. Voting has become, as H.L. Mencken said, just an advance auction on stolen goods.

For another thing, today, the United States is multicultural. America used to have its own distinct culture; the U.S. no longer stands for anything.

Race is just the most obvious thing that divides people. You can see that somebody's of a different race just by looking at them. The old saying about birds of a feather flocking together is basically true. It's very politically incorrect to make that observation, of course. Certainly if you're white. But it's factually accurate. Most things that are PC fly in the face of reality.

If people are of a different race, it increases the chances that they're not going to share other things. The key, for a rational person, is to judge people as individuals. Race, sex, religion, and cultural background are quick indicators of who a person might be. As are dress, accent, attitude, and what they say among many other indicators. You need as much data as you can get to help you judge what the other person will do, and who he is. It's actually quite stupid to not discriminate among people you encounter. But then the whole PC movement is quite stupid by its very nature.

But, back to the subject, you can't have a multicultural democracy. And you especially can't have one where the government is making laws that have to do with economics... where it allocates wealth from one group to another group.

So, sure. The U.S. is going to break apart, and you can certainly see it happening along racial lines. The active racism among many blacks isn't an anomaly.

Justin: I agree that racial tensions are rising in this country. But that's clearly not the only source of tension. What else might cause the U.S. to break apart?

Doug: Cultural differences.

The Pacific Northwest draws people who like the idea of ecotopia. Southern California draws a very different type of person than Northern California does. People that live in Las Vegas are quite different from the people that live in Omaha, and very different again from people that live in New York.

The U.S. has turned into a domestic empire. It's no longer the country that it was when it was founded. And the constitution itself has changed at least as much. It's a dead letter. Mainly window dressing. It's been interpreted out of existence.

Sure, the U.S. is going to break up; throughout history the colors of the map on the wall have always been running. I don't think the racial situation in the near term is going to get better. And the breakdown of the culture is definitely getting worse.

On the other hand, there's more racial intermingling and marriage now than there's ever been in the past. If we look down the road 1,000 years or so, racial distinctions will probably disappear. The average person will probably look like most Brazilians. Brazil, incidentally, is theoretically an integrated country—but there's still a huge amount of racism. Go farther into the future, when homo sapiens have conquered the planets and hopefully the stars, and we'll likely transform not only into new races, but new species. But I don't think any of us are looking that far ahead.

Justin: What about political tensions? Because, as I'm sure you've seen, the far-left and far-right are becoming more and more antagonistic. In some cases, they've even become violent towards each other.

Could radical political ideologies cause the country to break apart?

Doug: Yes, I think so.

In the late '60s and the early '70s, hundreds of bombings took place at universities, banks, and all kinds of places. The National Guard was in cities like Detroit during the riots, and they were raking buildings with .50 caliber machine guns. It was wild.

I don't think most remember this. At least, I don't see it being brought up anywhere.

I lived in Washington DC then. It seemed like there was tear gas in the air half the time I went out on a date on a Friday or Saturday night.

But as wild and wooly as things were back then, what we have now is much more serious.

The racial element is still there, but the ideological element is even more pronounced.

In those days, people at least talked to each other. You could have a disagreement, and it was a simple difference of opinion.

It's much worse now. Today, there's a visceral hatred between the left and the right, between the people that live in the so-called red counties and blue counties.

You add that to the racial situation. Then throw in the fact that the rich are getting richer at an exponential rate while the middle class is disappearing.

And let's not forget the large-scale subsidized migration of people from totally alien Third World hellholes. This is not what the U.S. was founded on. Before changes in the immigration law that were made in the '60s, immigrants were culturally compatible opportunity seekers that were coming to America to improve themselves.

Now, people from all kinds of alien places are being imported by the hundreds of thousands by NGOs; they then go on welfare in enclaves in different places around the country. This is unlikely to end well. The U.S. is no longer a country.

That said, I'm actually for open borders. But it's only possible if, A, there is zero welfare to attract the wrong types. And, B, all property was privately owned, to help ensure everyone is self-supporting.

Justin: But Doug, aren't you against large nation states? Would the Divided States of America be better?

Doug: Absolutely. In my ideal world, there would be approximately seven billion little nation states on the planet, all of them independent.

It would be excellent if the U.S. split into smaller entities, where the people that lived in these entities shared more in common with each other.

And let me go further. I think it was a mistake for the U.S. to have come together with the Constitution of 1789. The Articles of Confederation should have stayed in existence, with a few modifications. The Constitutional Convention of 1789 was actually a coup. A successful, non-violent coup. Most people didn't really care because the government was such a trivial factor in their lives in those days.

I'm just afraid that when the U.S. breaks up, which inevitably it will, it may not be peaceful. The existence of the USA—which is now just one of 200 other nation states, no longer anything special—is not part of the cosmic firmament. The original founding ideas of America expressed in the Declaration of Independence have been lost, washed away. The absence of those principles is why I say it's going to come to a bad end.

Justin: Do you think the United States will dissolve over time? Or will something set this in motion, possibly a financial or economic crisis?

Doug: An economic crisis always brings things to the fore.

When the standard of living is dropping, the government inevitably finds somebody or something to blame... anything other than itself.

Usually, they point the finger at foreigners. But if you get the wrong people in the government, they can point fingers at domestic enemies, the way the Germans did with the Jews in the '30s, or the way the Soviets did with the kulaks at the same time. Or the way the Chinese did with its enemies of the State under Mao. There are many, many other examples. Political power attracts the worst kind of people—and then brings out the worst in them.

Economic turmoil causes social turmoil and political turmoil. And one of the things that scares me most is that if things get spooky within the U.S., people in the government will try to find a foreign enemy in order to "unite" the country.

Incidentally, I don't feel that uniting the country is necessarily a good idea. It all depends on which direction they're united towards, and united against what. And do the people of the United States have enough in common anymore to even be united? I think not, in an age of multiculturalism.

There are a lot of problems, and they're bubbling to the surface. When the economy gets bad, which it will, I think the pot will boil over.

Doug Casey on Puerto Rico's Debt

ORIGINALLY PUBLISHED ON NOVEMBER 1, 2017

Justin's note: Puerto Rico's economy is in shambles. It's been this way for years. But the situation went from bad to catastrophic when Hurricane Maria rocked the tiny island in late September 2017. The situation is now so bad that Donald Trump's talking about wiping out Puerto Rico's debt. That would be unprecedented...

Justin: Doug, what do you make of Trump's suggestion? Could he really wipe out Puerto Rico's debt?

Doug: I don't know about the legality of Trump—as opposed to the Puerto Rico legislature—defaulting on the debt. But it's not just a reasonable suggestion, but a good idea, and probably inevitable. I mean this tiny island of three million owes over $100 billion—about $70 billion in balance sheet debt plus another $30 billion of off-balance sheet pension liabilities. And probably a lot more in contingent liabilities, guarantees, and what-have-you. How are they supposed to pay that back?

Let's do the math on this. Divide three million into 100 billion, and you come up with around $33,000 per person.

But that's sugarcoating it. Because only a million people on the island work—being very liberal with the concept of employment. If you use this figure, the debt comes to about $100,000 per person.

It's completely impossible for them to pay off this debt. Especially since it's the poorest and most socialist-leaning part of the U.S. So, yes. Puerto Rico will default, one way or another. And it should default.

Justin: What about Puerto Rican bondholders? Are you sympathetic towards them?

Doug: These people were paid handsomely to subsidize the Puerto Rican government in a co-dependent relationship for many years. And they were very well paid with high tax-free income for years to facilitate San Juan politicians bribing local voters to re-elect them.

They assumed that the U.S. government would step in and bail them out, rather than allow sovereign default.

So, they should be punished for subsidizing the stupidity of the Puerto Rican government for all these years. I have zero sympathy for them.

So yeah, default on the bonds. Because if you don't, you're absolutely putting an albatross—it's an anvil, actually—around the neck of the productive part of that economy to pay off those bonds.

But that's just one reason to default. Another is that all that debt guarantees that future generations of Puerto Rican residents will be turned into indentured servants to pay it off.

A third reason is that it should ruin the Puerto Rican government's credit rating for a while, which will preclude them from borrowing again. That's a good thing. Government spending is almost all consumption—it siphons capital from the productive private sector, dissipates capital, and lowers the standard of living.

Justin: And a default would be in Puerto Rico's best interest?

Doug: Yes, for the reasons I mentioned. The moral and economically intelligent thing to do is to default on the bonds. There should be no aid from the U.S. to Puerto Rico. It would mostly go to putting in new infrastructure. Which means the electricity and water would work again, and favored contractors would get rich. But that wouldn't solve any of the island's real problems—bureaucracy, corruption, high taxes, and a socialist mentality.

Tourists will come back to the waterlogged and mildewed hotels at some point, I suppose. But the island isn't cheap even in good times, since everything is imported. The only reason to be there is to take advantage of those provisions in their tax code—Acts 20 and 22, that may let an American live there tax-free.

There's no real economic activity on the island besides tourism. Even the drug companies—which were quite big employers for many years—are leaving. So, there are going to be scores of thousands of unemployed waiters, maids, and taxi drivers for quite a while.

Justin: But Doug, Puerto Rico is a U.S. territory. Shouldn't the federal government have its back?

Doug: No. Puerto Rico should actually be an independent country. Historically, that's what Puerto Ricans have always wanted, since we took it from the Spaniards as a spoil of war in 1898. Although in recent years, Puerto Ricans have gotten so used to the welfare bennies and convenience of being part of the U.S. that few want independence anymore. Half of them now live in the continental U.S. A pity. It could become the most prosperous country in the Western Hemisphere if they pursued the right policies. It could turn itself into the next Hong Kong or Singapore.

But that won't happen. That's because the island's ethos is very welfare-oriented. It's been totally corrupted by being owned and treated as a U.S. colony for the last 100 years. At least as far back as *West Side Story*, which was done in the 1950s, the place was a laughing stock. I love that song that Maria's friend sings. She says, "Puerto Rico, my heart's devotion, let it sink back in the ocean."

Most of the smart and entrepreneurial Puerto Ricans have long since hightailed it to New York or Miami.

The island is culturally, linguistically, and ethnically different from the rest of the U.S.—it makes no more sense to be part of the U.S. than would other Caribbean or Latin countries. That sort of thing is what signals the difference between a cohesive country, and an empire. The U.S. resembles an empire more and more as time goes by.

I'd love to see them become independent and wealthy, in the manner of Hong Kong or Singapore. But they'll probably devolve into just another Latin American money pit. I don't know what the answer is—in fact, there is no answer. The place has been corrupted by over a century of welfare. It's got to change its culture, and that isn't easy. But it shouldn't be your problem, my problem, or the problem of other Americans.

Justin: I hate to say it but you're probably right. The chances of Puerto Rico becoming the next Hong Kong or Singapore are slim to none.

But let's pretend you're in charge of Puerto Rico. How would you start the rebuilding process? How would you turn it into the next Hong Kong?

Doug: After defaulting on all the government debt to clear the deck? I would then abolish all welfare programs, of whatever nature, for both individuals and corporations. I'd get rid of their local income tax and all regulations of whatever description.

If you want it to boom like Hong Kong or Singapore, you have to put the same conditions that those places have in place. And those are the conditions.

It's necessary to totally free marketize the place. That would attract companies and entrepreneurs from all over the world. Institute gold as money. Further, I'd take all the government's assets—of any type, including national sovereignty—and put them in a corporation, distributing publicly listed shares to the citizens.

Theoretically, the people own the government and its assets. But that's a meaningless concept, unless you can take that dead capital public in major stock markets.

The government wouldn't do anything but provide police and a court system. But, perversely, those two things are too important to leave to the type of people that wind up working for the government—they always become centers of corruption. They should be privatized too.

There's a lot more to say about this plan—it's something I've been trying to sell to failing states for many years now. It would be a total non-starter in Puerto Rico, simply because it's part of the U.S.

The place doesn't need some changes around the edges. It needs total and radical reform, top to bottom. And it could become—very quickly—the leading edge of the entire world's economy. It could be turned into Dubai on steroids. But it won't be. Well, as Einstein said, after hydrogen, stupidity is the most common thing in the universe.

Justin: You tried this sort of thing in Haiti and a few other Third World countries. How'd those trips go? Do the leaders of these places actually follow your advice?

Doug: They always listen, if only because they're desperate. This has long been one of my hobbies—going to backward, worthless dystopian Third World countries, places much worse off than Puerto Rico.

Most recently, I tried this in Haiti, which I've been to numerous times over the last 40 years. But these places are all the same in that they're kleptocracies, where people use the government as a formal, organized vehicle for enriching themselves. They're uninterested in change. Except the Haitians, like the Puerto Ricans, would also like to become a U.S. state.

But sure, I've had very entertaining experiences in many countries around the world. That would be a subject for another conversation, for a book actually. I should write a book about these adventures before I forget all the details.

Justin: I can't imagine Haiti's actually trying any of this. Are they?

Doug: No. Forget about it. I mean the individuals, the guys that I actually talked to in the president's office, weren't stupid. They could understand this.

But they're making so much money stealing now... change is the last thing they want. Even offering them the opportunity to make 10 times as much legitimately doesn't entice them—the idea of possibly losing what they are stealing now and breaking a bunch of other people's rice bowls scared them too much.

Although, I thought I came close in a couple of places…

Justin: Do you plan to try this in any other countries? If so, what might be your next stop?

Doug: Will I try to do this again? I don't know. If somebody gives me a good introduction to a president somewhere I suppose I'll get on a plane. Can't help myself when I see a neat adventure.

If I did, it'll probably be someplace in Africa. But frankly, I've kind of been there and done that. I've pitched this idea to the governments of a dozen countries around the world. It's been a fun hobby. But after a while, you see one hellhole, you've seen them all.

Justin: Well, be sure to let us know if you do take another stab at this. Thank you for your time.

Doug: Sure thing, Justin.

Doug Casey on the Recent NFL Protests

ORIGINALLY PUBLISHED ON OCTOBER 20, 2017

Justin's note: The NFL protests this season have become one of today's most controversial topics. Everyone had something to say about them. Even Donald Trump's up in arms over it... I still can't help but wonder if people should even care about this. Here's Doug's take on the matter...

Justin: Doug, I can't wait to get your take on the recent NFL protests. But first tell me what you think of the National Anthem. Is it a worthy tradition?

Doug: I don't see what sporting events have to do with nationalism. I don't think they should go together.

The idea of playing a national anthem at sporting events or other gatherings is foolish and dangerous. It elevates the notion of the state, it keeps the presence of the government in front of people. It's almost as bad an idea as having kids pledge allegiance to the flag at the start of the school day—another fairly recent innovation.

I looked into the history of this, and the anthem apparently first started being played sporadically at baseball games, during World War 1. It only turned into a tradition during WW2. Needless to say, during the '30s, the Germans, the Italians, and the Russians always used their anthems to get the crowd thinking in the mode of "nationalistic citizens" watching the home team battle the enemy team, as opposed to sports fans just out to watch a game and have a good time.

Playing the National Anthem before a game is a bad idea. But every country in the world does it now. I think the crowds generally dislike it as a distraction and a waste of time, but nobody will say anything for fear of being lambasted for being "unpatriotic." It's groupthink in action.

Apart from the fact that anthems all sound discordant, and grate against the ear drum. They're all basically military music—which is itself a contradictory term. I'll only except the Marseillaise—which really is a noble tune, but inappropriate for U.S. audiences.

Ultimately, it's up to the team and stadium owners. If they want to do it, that's their business. But it's become such a tradition that—especially in view of the U.S. being constantly involved in a war somewhere—it's likely going to be impossible to eradicate. It no longer matters that it's a bad tradition—it's now a tradition.

And let me go further. I think that it's in very bad taste and negative influence for the U.S. government and the U.S. military to use football games for military display. Flying fighter planes around and having military bands marching, is much more what I'd expect of the Germans in the '30s than an ostensibly peaceful country in today's world.

That said, I think that it makes sense to show respect for things like the National Anthem. They're part of the national ethos. Disrespecting them upsets a community at a very gut level; it's unwise, like telling someone his mother is ugly and has low morals.

Justin: Are you saying NFL players shouldn't protest by taking a knee?

Doug: Well, anybody has a right to do anything, as long as it doesn't aggress against other persons or their property. But just because something is legal and moral doesn't mean it can't also be stupid.

I'm not even sure what point these players are trying to make. In some cases, these athletes are making tens of millions of dollars a year. These guys are young, rich, famous, good-looking and generally on top of the world. They're not subjects of "discrimination."

So, why are they doing this? Do they feel that they're actually in some danger of being shot? The answer is no, unless they're hanging out in the ghetto, or acting out as thugs somewhere—some of them do. There's certainly no reason to think these guys are moral paradigms. The rates of spousal abuse and off-field violence in the NFL—which is about 70% black—are way above the norm. The guy who started this nonsense, Colin Kaepernick, is actually just a scam artist. A crybaby looking for attention.

Frankly, I don't care what they do or feel. It's foolish and in bad taste for them to use their athletic platform to say whatever they're saying. It's unclear to me exactly what they're trying to say.

Justin: You're right, Doug. Colin Kaepernick was the first player to make this protest. He did so last year before a preseason game. And he kneeled to take a stand against police brutality and racial injustice.

Now you have entire teams doing it. Could these "showings of unity" repair race relations in this country?

Doug: No. Instead, they will damage race relations further.

The problem is that people are genetically programmed to be suspicious of those of a different race or even a different community.

A couple hundred thousand years ago, you're out hunting a deer. If you met somebody else out there hunting that deer, and he wasn't part of your immediate clan, he was probably an enemy. There's a good chance that he was going to kill you after the deer goes down. The more different he was, the greater the odds violence would ensue.

Racism isn't abnormal or unnatural. It's actually a primitive survival characteristic. It's perfectly normal, from an evolutionary or genetic point of view. In fact, birds of a feather flock together, and like attracts like. If you're walking down a lonely city side street at night, who's more likely to give you trouble: Some young Jews going to a chess club meeting, or some young blacks going to a bar?

Of course, we discriminate, based on whatever factors are relevant. It's stupid not to. But race is just the first filter. There are many others. The key to intelligent and moral action is to treat people as individuals, not as members of groups, whenever possible. Just the opposite of what so-called "identity politics" is all about. They see people primarily as members of racial, ethnic, linguistic, sexual, or other groups.

I prefer to deal with people as individuals. If they're black, homosexual, Muslim, or what-have-you that gives me more information about them—information that may or may not be relevant. Only fools and idiots disregard facts because they seem politically incorrect.

And that leads me back to what these players are doing. It's part of the whole identity-politics movement.

They don't see other people as individuals. They see them as members of groups. And when you see people as members of groups, you're asking for conflict.

The solution is to see people as individuals, not as members of groups. But these guys see themselves as members of a group—they're actually being overtly racist. Even the white guys on the team—they're feeling, not thinking. Showing solidarity with their black teammates, even though the whole exercise is idiotic on every level.

Like I said, though racism is natural, it's increasingly rather stupid in today's high-tech world. These guys are being counterproductive—but perhaps they're harbingers of the future. A guy I used to know, Michael Hart, used to come to our Eris Society meetings in Aspen. One, among other books, he wrote, was *The 100: A Ranking Of The Most Influential Persons In History*. A speech he gave one year was about how the US was going to break up into smaller countries, and part of it would be on racial lines. At the time, I thought that unlikely. Now I think Michael may have been right...

Justin: Should NFL owners be able to fire employees who engage in these protests?

Doug: Absolutely. Look, you've got a right to your political opinions. Or any other opinions. But if you work for an organization, you must act under the terms and conditions that are set down. If you don't like it, quit.

If the owner of the team doesn't like your actions, opinions, beliefs, attitudes, or just the way you look, he has every right to fire you, for any reason.

You don't own your job. The two of you must arrive at an agreement as to how you're going to relate. Giving workers "rights" that don't exist is only a cause for even more conflict. Relationships must be based on pure voluntarism.

So, it's perfectly fine to fire somebody for any cause, or no cause at all, and that includes their beliefs and opinions—or race or religion. Beliefs, opinions, race and religion aren't sacred, nor should they be grounds for legal action.

The only place where people are "equal" is in a court of law. Anything goes in commercial relations. You don't have a right to your job. The very concept is both morally repugnant and economically stupid.

Justin: So, this sort of seems like a non-issue. And yet, everyday Americans are losing their minds over this. What do you make of that?

Doug: I'm afraid that although the average person may or may not do tolerably well running his own life, he's totally incompetent at things beyond his personal life. They know vastly more about the Kardashians, sports, and maybe astrology than anything of importance. That's an argument against democracy, of course, which is a bit off-topic at the moment.

The problem is that most people don't have the knowledge they need for making "public policy" decisions to start with. And when they're confronted with decisions, or have to form opinions, they do it on the basis of what they feel, not what they think. And they don't know the difference.

Justin: What about Donald Trump? Should he concern himself with this?

Doug: Well, Donald Trump is not a libertarian. He's an authoritarian.

On top of that, he's a nationalist. So, as a jingoist, of course he's upset over this—but it's unseemly to be running around hooting and panting like a chimpanzee.

I find it inappropriate. He shouldn't have anything to do with it at all. It's none of his business, either as a private citizen or as president. But he clearly wants to proclaim some *diktat* on the matter that everyone has to obey.

NFL football is a private sporting event. It's between the players and the owners. Let them work it out. It's got nothing to do with the US government.

Frankly, I'd rather see the Salvation Army band than the Marine Corps band. They're less militaristic and less likely to get people riled up looking for a war. Even if they happen to play "Onward Christian Soldiers."

Justin: Well, I think that covers everything I wanted to ask. So, thank you for sharing your insights again, Doug.

Doug: You're welcome, Justin.

Doug Casey on Catalonia's Independence

ORIGINALLY PUBLISHED ON OCTOBER 16, 2017

Justin's note: Catalonia wants independence. As you probably know, Catalonia—the richest region of Spain—held a referendum on October 1. And the people voted overwhelmingly in favor of independence. It's now likely only a matter of time before Catalonia breaks off from the rest of the country. When that happens, it will have serious ramifications for all of Europe…

Justin: Doug, the Catalans want to break off from Spain. Are you surprised by this?

Doug: No. But very pleased to hear it. As you know, all of these European nation states were cobbled together from small kingdoms and miscellaneous ethnic groups. They were put together either by force and conquest, or the marriage of some ruler, with no consent of the ruled. National boundaries aren't part of the cosmic firmament; they're fluid.

Spain is not a natural entity. Neither is France, Italy, Germany, or even Britain, for that matter. People don't realize it, but up until about 100 years ago the people of Spain mostly spoke mutually unintelligible dialects. The Catalans speak a different language today. The Basques, who are north of the Catalans, are another culturally distinct group with a language that's totally unrelated to any other in Europe. Spain is a legal fiction that actually just benefits the big shots in Madrid.

The people of different regions don't have all that much in common. And yet, they've been put together in a nation state—one of humanity's more stupid and destructive inventions.

So, I expect the devolution of both Spain and Europe to continue.

Justin: Why do you reject the idea of a nation state?

Doug: Well, let me first identify my preferences. The optimal situation for the world economy isn't the more-or-less 225 nation states we have today. It's about seven billion little nation states.

I'd like to see everyone completely independent. The state serves very little useful purpose. Throughout history its main products have been wars, taxes, pogroms, revolutions, persecutions, confiscations, and the like. Politics produces nothing; it's all about who decides who gets what at whose expense. Political entities are coercive by their nature. The bigger they are, the more dysfunctional. Nation-states are just a testimony to how thoughtless the average person is, that he accedes to the idea, like a sheep. So, seeing Spain break apart is a step in the right direction.

But it's not just where I hope things go—it's also where things are, in fact, going to go. Even in Europe, with the oldest and most powerful nation-states, you have scores of serious independence movements right now.

Hopefully, it will vanquish the silly idea that "unity" is a value, a good thing. That's as stupid as the idea that its opposite, "diversity" is good. They're just political notions, neither good nor bad. They're just tools to influence the emotions of the *hoi polloi*. Who benefits from the unity of Spain? Certainly not the average Catalan.

But there are lots of secession movements in Europe—scores of them. It's not just the Catalans, or the Scots and the Welsh in the United Kingdom. Small places like the Faroe Islands, which are part of Denmark, might break off too. And they'd be very wise to do so. Take a look at the map on the following page.

In Italy, it's not just the area of Veneto around Venice, and Lombardy around Milan. Sicily, Sardinia, South Tyrol, and Friuli, the area around Trieste, all have secession movements. Before Garibaldi and Victor Emmanuel came on the scene, before unification in 1870, Italy was dozens of little kingdoms and duchies. It could go back to that today.

People don't realize that even the Italian language really didn't exist not so long ago. "Italian" was scores of dialects. It only started to crystalize with Dante's Divina Commedia. Northern Italians not only couldn't understand southern Italians speaking their own versions of Italian, they were different ethnic groups. Even today the northern Italians look down on the southern Italians and call them African Italians.

Same thing with Germany. Germany used to be dozens of baronies, dukedoms, principalities and what-have-you before Bismarck. The world would have been better off if it had stayed that way. A united Germany turned out to be a very bad idea.

The colors of the map on the wall are always running. They have been since Roman times, and they'll continue to do so. And the fact of the matter is that, unstable as it is, Europe is among the most stable places in the world. Every single country in Africa, the Middle East, and central Asia is a completely artificial construct where the lines of the map were drawn completely artificially in a boardroom in Europe. National boundaries exist with no attention paid to the ethnicity, religion, language, or the customs of the local people.

You're going to see lots of borders violently readjusted in these places in the years to come. Hopefully, Catalonia will be non-violent.

Justin: So, if this is just the beginning, what European country will start to break apart next? Any guesses?

Doug: A guess? Belgium, the very homeland of the EU, should be at least two countries, tomorrow morning. It came into being during the Napoleonic era. The Flemish in the north should be in Flanders, and the Walloons in the south should be in Wallonia. They're linguistically and ethnically quite different.

The Basques, both in France and Spain, are an ethnically, linguistically, culturally different group. They should leave. And the Scots would do well to get away from Britain. Generally, it's the most productive parts of a country that don't like being exploited by the poorer, non-productive parts.

But about Catalonia, it seems the people most opposed to leaving Spain are, surprisingly, the most free-market-oriented types. This is because the Catalan independence politicians are all hard-core socialists and communists. And although it's a good thing economically for Catalonia to be independent—they now apparently ship two tax dollars to Madrid for every dollar of benefit they get in return—it will be a bit inconvenient in other ways. It will be disastrous if they try to turn it into a socialist people's republic, because that's the way these politicians are oriented.

Of course, all European politicians are socialists at heart. Most politicians everywhere are. Some populist is always itching to try out his version of social engineering on the public. So, he's likely to be most pro-independence, in order to become an international big shot. Most of the resistance knows that Catalonia will become much more left-leaning and collectivist if it becomes independent.

That's the case everywhere. There really are no free-market-oriented independence movements, which is the real pity. Most of these places are very nationalistic and socialist-leaning. The dark side of human nature to the fore.

But, you know, the first step is to break up large dysfunctional groups into smaller and less dysfunctional ones. Eventually some of them will turn free market just out of necessity. If you had seven billion nation states, none of them would be socialist—you can't exploit yourself. People might come to realize the state is just a fraud, where everyone tries to live at the expense of everyone else.

And let me emphasize that I'm not saying that new states are good in themselves—they're not. They're just much better than the status quo. The best outcome would be autonomous regions, controlled by market forces, not political forces. There's absolutely no good or service that wouldn't be provided by entrepreneurs. Especially in today's high-tech world, a state bureaucracy is unnecessary for anything that's wanted or needed.

Justin: What investment implications, if any, do you see coming out of this?

Doug: What are the implications indeed? In a chaotic environment, especially where nationalist and socialist ideas are the minds of all these politicians, it doesn't augur well for the value of property. In other words, if it was a free-market secession movement, asset prices in Catalonia would soar; billions of dollars would try to get into the place. But it's a nationalist/socialist movement—so billions are going to try to get out. It's going to hurt the value of local assets.

So, this could present an excellent opportunity to pick up companies and real estate in these countries, because fear is going to reign.

What are these people going to do once they become independent? Try to become Hong Kong, or try to become Cuba? Maybe there will be a civil war like there was in the 1930s, because Catalonia is the most productive part of Spain, and Madrid doesn't want to see the revenue go away. Barcelona doesn't want to be Madrid's milk cow. Anything is possible in today's world.

Justin: What about the euro, the currency of Spain and the rest of the European Union (EU)?

Doug: Well, the euro has been a dead man walking since the day it was created. It can only be described as an Esperanto currency. It can't possibly hold together.

You can't have a currency that's unbacked by anything, but used by countries with vastly differing economies, welfare traditions, and so forth. The stronger secessionist movements become, the weaker the euro will become.

The Euro is a dead duck; it will turn into wallpaper, like hundreds of paper currencies before it. These countries are going to go back to their individual currencies. Actually, you're going to see gold once again used as a day-to-day currency. It will be facilitated in that role by the cryptocurrency revolution.

People forget that during the 19th century—which was the most stable, prosperous, peaceful century in human history—the lira, the franc, the mark, the pound, and the ruble were all just names for certain amounts of gold. All of these countries issued small gold coins and they were completely interchangeable across borders. So, hopefully we'll go back to that.

Justin: That's yet another reason to own gold. Anyway, that's everything I wanted to ask you today. So, once again, thank you for sharing your insights.

Doug: My pleasure.

Doug Casey on Why Bitcoin Is Money

―――

ORIGINALLY PUBLISHED ON SEPTEMBER 21, 2017

Justin's note: Cryptocurrencies are on fire. Every investor is now wondering if this mania has legs, or if it's a bubble that's about to burst. Doug's been on the winning side of more manias than we can count. He was also an early investor in bitcoin...

Justin: Doug, you've owned Bitcoin for some time now. How'd you get started in cryptocurrencies?

Doug: I was first introduced to them several years ago in Cafayate, Argentina. A lot of interesting people come through town.

A young Belgian guy came to visit, and I bought him lunch, and we discussed Bitcoin. He was a very early enthusiast. Because I bought him lunch, he gave me a physical Bitcoin as a souvenir. They actually exist. They're collectibles that have the codes inscribed on them.

I still have that Bitcoin. At the time, a Bitcoin was worth $13. Now, they're trading for about $4,000.

So, for that reason, that was the cheapest lunch I ever bought anyone. I wish I had listened to his argument, because I could have made millions. About 300-1 over just a few years...

Justin: Yeah, it's crazy how much Bitcoin's run over the last few years.

Do you think it's headed even higher? Or is it a bubble about to burst?

Doug: I'm suspicious of where Bitcoin currently trades. The bright side is that there will never be more than 21 million created. I understand that only about half of them have come into existence.

And there are only about 25 million people in the world that own Bitcoin right now.

That's a tiny proportion of the people in the world, and it's going to grow. There's going to be a lot more buying of Bitcoins and other cryptocurrencies simply because so few people own them right now, and there's good reason to own them.

Justin: I agree that the market for cryptocurrencies will get bigger. But why exactly?

Doug: Cryptocurrencies are only the first and most obvious application of blockchain technology.

I'm not a computer jock, but that's unimportant when it comes to seeing the implications of the technology—much as it was unnecessary to be either a driver or a mechanic 100 years ago to appreciate the merits of the automobile. It's been said that the blockchain technology may be the most important single development since the invention of the internet itself.

It's going to change the way documents are transmitted, the way real estate is sold and registered, the way stocks and bonds are tracked, the way inventory is tracked. It's a game changer in many ways.

As far as the cryptocurrencies are concerned, my original objection to Bitcoin was that it's not backed by anything. So, it's really a fiat currency. It's very much like the US dollar, the Zambian Kwacha, the Argentine peso, or any of the other 150-plus currencies in today's world. It's a floating abstraction.

But I missed something when I said, back then, that it had no value. It's a fiat currency, but it has much more value than any other.

Justin: And what did you miss?

Doug: Aristotle defined the five characteristics of good money in the 4th century BC. And his analysis is as accurate now as it was then. It must be durable, divisible, convenient, consistent, and have use value in and of itself. Based on that, Aristotle believed gold and silver were best suited for use as money. Let's analyze how Bitcoin does by these five criteria.

Durable. Bitcoin and other cryptocurrencies are definitely durable, unless we have an electromagnetic pulse (EMP) or a significant solar flare that wipes out all the computers. They're not as durable as the metals, but they're adequate, barring a collapse of civilization.

Divisible. They're infinitely divisible. Better than the physical metals—although the metals can be accounted in tiny fractions too.

Convenient. Yes—as long as you have a smartphone, Bitcoin is very convenient. But your smartphone, or something like it, may not always be with you. And your counterparty also has to have one. And it's not very convenient if someone doesn't know or trust Bitcoin. Right now, that's probably 98% of humanity.

Consistent. Absolutely. Every Bitcoin is exactly like another one. It's at least as good as .999 fine gold that way.

The problem I had with Bitcoin to start with was the fifth point: does it have use value in itself, so you can't get stuck holding the bag?

If you have a million US dollars and nobody accepts them, they have no use in and of themselves. They're just unsecured liabilities of a bankrupt government. Like a million Zimbabwe dollars. And a fiat currency is easily destroyed by its issuer. The things are burning matches. They have half-lives, like radioactive elements.

And I said that was the problem with Bitcoin. But I was wrong about that.

Bitcoin is certainly a fiat currency like the dollar or the Kwacha. But it's also an excellent transfer device. You can move wealth from one country to another, or to another person, quickly and privately. I'd say secretly, but you're not supposed to say "secret" anymore, you can only say "private." <u>Part of the politically correct corruption of language</u>[1], I might add.

And you can do so outside of the banking system, which is increasingly important.

Hopefully, among other things, blockchain and Bitcoin are going to destroy the SWIFT system, which is expensive (at least $50-100 per transaction), slow (generally a day or two, sometimes a week or more), and insecure (who trusts either big banks or the US Government?). And SWIFT requires that all dollars clear through New York.

[Editor's note: SWIFT is used by thousands of banks around the world to send payment instructions worth trillions of dollars each day.]

So, this is the use value of Bitcoin. It allows you to transfer something that is accepted as money outside of the banking system, and outside of fiat money currencies.

Justin: Would you go as far as to call it money?

Doug: Sure, because what is money? Money is a medium of exchange and a store of value. So, almost anything can be used as money. Some things are just much better than others.

Salt, seashells, and cows have all historically been used as money. After all, the

---

1. www.caseyresearch.com/doug-casey-on-the-political-correctness-movement/

word pecuniary comes from the Latin pecus, which means cow. And salary comes from the Latin sal, which is salt. Wampum were seashells. Cigarettes are money in prisons and war zones. Even giant Yap island discs have been used as money.

Anything can be a medium of exchange, as long as it's accepted. And Bitcoin increasingly is. It fulfills that—or is in process of doing so. It will become more and more accepted as most government fiat currencies approach their intrinsic values—essentially zero—over the next business cycle.

Justin: What about as a store of value?

Doug: Well, this is more of a problem. You've got two kinds of currencies: commodity currencies and fiat currencies.

The commodity currencies are physical commodities. You know they have use value. Fiat currencies, on the other hand, are just made up. They're totally arbitrary.

It's like that joke about sardines. You've got eating sardines and trading sardines. Commodity currencies are like eating sardines. Fiat currencies are like trading sardines. Of course, there's no guarantee that Bitcoin is going to be accepted a year or two from now; if it's not, it fails the store of value test. But it's accepted at the moment. And it's been growing in value at a spectacular rate—unlike fiat currencies, which have all been falling against real goods and services at about 5-10% a year. Incidentally, I don't put much faith in the accuracy of government inflation figures.

But Bitcoin is a technological innovation. There might be Bitcoin 2.0 and 3.0. What will the current Bitcoin then be worth? There's a reason the expression "High tech, big wreck" is true. Just because so far it's been a great speculation doesn't mean it's a good store of value. Technology, a solar flare, or even government action could wipe it out.

The bottom line, Bitcoin passes the medium of exchange test for the moment and store of value test for the moment. So you can definitely say it's money—for the moment. But so's the Argentine peso. I have little confidence Bitcoin will be here say five years from now.

Doug Casey on How High Bitcoin Could Go

ORIGINALLY PUBLISHED ON SEPTEMBER 22, 2017

Justin's note: Doug explains bitcoin's upside potential…

Justin: Doug, you told me how a young Belgian man gifted you a bitcoin. Have you bought any more since then?

Doug: Yes. I've put $100,000 in them. It's no longer early days, that's for sure. But perhaps it's like getting into the Internet stocks back in 1998—they weren't cheap, but the bubble got much, much bigger. And the Internet—contrary to what people like Paul Krugman thought—was not itself a bubble. Up till now, the only way to play this has been the coins, the tokens, like Bitcoin.

Justin: Got it. Do you own any other cryptos?

Doug: Yeah, I've got Ethereum, and a couple of others as speculations. There are perhaps a thousand of them out there now, and most of them are garbage.

So, I'm getting involved in these cryptocurrencies on several levels. I'm trying to make the trend my friend. But cautiously, because there's a lot of speculation going on.

And as you know, the Chinese are clamping down on the area right now—but that's going to change.

Justin: It doesn't seem like you're too concerned about all this bubble talk then.

Doug: Not true. I am concerned. The market is very, very bubbly. But I think it's going higher, for several reasons. One, as we discussed, is that some of the cryptos have great utility, and only about 25 million out of the 7 billion people in the world have them. They're going to get much bigger in the developed world, but even bigger in the Third World.

In all of Africa, most of South America, and a great part of Asia, fiat currencies issued by governments are a joke. They're extremely unreliable within those countries. And they're totally worthless outside the physical borders of the country. That's why those people want dollars.

I think that the Third World will adopt Bitcoin and some other coins in a huge way.

This is because people who own cryptocurrencies, at least for the time being, are making money. They're saving an appreciating asset rather than a depreciating asset. You're on a Sisyphean treadmill if you try to save a Third World currency—but ¾ of humanity have no alternative.

These coins are also private. They can transfer wealth outside of the country, which is very helpful. Kwachas, pulas, pesos, and such are worthless outside of the country that issues them. Of course, governments hate that, and this will present a big problem down the road.

The whole Third World is going to go to these cryptocurrencies. They all have smartphones in these countries. A phone is the first thing they buy after food and clothing.

Sure, it's a bubbly market. But soon billions more people will be participating in it. So, it's going to get more bubbly. That's my argument.

Justin: I've never heard that argument before, but it makes a lot of sense.

So, do you view cryptos mainly as speculation? Or do you also see them as a chaos hedge?

Doug: Well like I said, cryptocurrencies are just the first application of block-chain technology[1]. I think they have staying power simply because government fiat currencies are bad, and will be getting worse. They're not going away. But I view them mainly as a speculative opportunity right now.

How high is Bitcoin going to go? Bitcoin is kind of the numeraire. It's the gold standard, as it were, of cryptocurrencies. John McAfee, who founded the cyber security giant McAfee, Inc., thinks it's headed much higher.

I recently got together with John. I stayed at his house, we spent a day together, had drinks and cigars, and got along extremely well. He's a very, very bright, knowledgeable, and entertaining guy.

He thinks Bitcoin's going to $50,000.

---

1. www.caseyresearch.com/doug-casey-on-why-bitcoin-is-money/

That sounds outrageous, but it's entirely possible. Another 10-1 in a manic market is possible—this brings up thoughts of tulip bulbs, of course.

Remember, Central Banks all over the world are printing up fiat currencies by the trillions, desperately trying to put off a collapse of the world economy. Many will issue their own cryptos—they're trying to totally abolish paper cash as we speak. And they won't want competition from private currencies like Bitcoin. Governments may well try to outlaw peer-to-peer cryptos. But that's another topic.

Justin: Very exciting stuff. But I need to ask you one last thing before I let you go… How do Bitcoin and these cryptocurrencies relate to gold? Are they good or bad for gold?

I'm sure many of our readers are wondering this, too.

Doug: They're very good for gold. Extremely good. That's because they're drawing attention to the nature of the monetary system. That's something few people think about. At all.

When people buy these cryptocurrencies, even if they know nothing about hard money, economics, or monetary theory, they inevitably ask themselves, "Hmm, Bitcoin or the dollar?" They're both currencies. Then they can start asking questions about the nature of the dollar… the nature of inflation… and whether the dollar has any real value, and what's going to happen to it, and why.

People are going to start asking themselves these questions—which wouldn't have occurred to them otherwise. They're going to see that only a certain number of Bitcoin will ever be issued. But dollars can be created by the trillions, by the hundreds of trillions.

That's going to make them very suspicious of the dollar. It's going to get a lot of people thinking about money and economics in a way that they never thought about it before. And this is inevitably going to lead them to gold.

So, the Bitcoin and cryptocurrency revolution will prove extremely valuable for gold. It's going to draw the attention of millions, or hundreds of millions of people, to gold as the real alternative to the dollar and other currencies, after Bitcoin.

Plus, I suspect future versions of Bitcoin, or Bitcoin 2.0, will be easily redeemable in gold grams. So, this is actually a big deal that most people aren't looking at.

Justin: That makes a lot of sense, but I don't think most people view cryptos this way. They see cryptos as a threat to gold, rather than something that could send gold much higher.

But anyway, that's everything I wanted to ask you today. So, thank you for sharing those unique insights.

Doug: Sure, any time.

[Editor's note: To hear more from Doug on why Bitcoin will drive gold to all-time highs, check out this new video[2].]

2. www.youtube.com/watch?v=tS8p5JamWhE&t=27s

Doug Casey on What Will Trigger Bitcoin's Collapse

ORIGINALLY PUBLISHED ON DECEMBER 21, 2017

Justin's note: Central bankers are losing sleep over bitcoin. And they should be. It's a direct threat to their monopoly on money. Because of this, they're trying everything they can to crush bitcoin. They're urging people not to buy it. They're calling it a bubble. They're even talking about launching their own rival digital currencies. Here's what Doug Casey has to say about this…

Justin: Doug, governments around the world seem to be waging a war on bitcoin. Do you see expect to see more of this in the years ahead?

Doug: Absolutely. You can plan your life around governments doing everything they can to discourage not only bitcoin, but all the other private cryptocurrencies as well.

It will be for pretty much the same reasons they hate gold, and other hard moneys. The State believes the issuance of currency is one of its major prerogatives, like making war and levying taxes. It's critical to them not to have alternatives, competition, when it comes to money.

For one thing, almost every government in the world is running deficits—gigantic deficits in many cases. They're financing those deficits by printing money. It's national policy everywhere because they believe deficits "stimulate" the economy as a bonus.

Most of that newly created money is flowing into the stock, bond markets, and real estate markets. It's making everybody feel much wealthier. Except for the bottom 50%—they're getting poorer.

Government and central banks don't want to give up that monopoly on money.

Least of all the US, since our major export isn't wheat or airplanes—it's dollars. So, they're going to do what they can to quash bitcoin and the others. For a myriad of reasons.

Justin: But will they succeed?

Doug: Well, they could certainly illegalize it. But would that eliminate it? About as well as their laws eliminated drugs or prostitution today. Or alcohol during the '20s. Fat chance. Although illegalization would certainly make cryptos inconvenient and risky.

But could they destroy cryptos? Who knows what kind of computing power the National Security Agency (NSA) has. They might be able to destroy any computer network or digital product at this point.

This is a huge argument against any kind of purely electronic currency—anything can happen in the ether.

Bitcoin is evidence of a worldwide distrust in government fiat currencies, though. And they're right to be distrustful; I don't doubt that we'll experience monetary chaos in the future.

At some point, they'll try to ban bitcoin, though. They'll tell people it's the law that they have to use the national e-currency. Plus they'll use moral suasion and propaganda. You know the drill. They'll say if you use bitcoin you're a money launderer, a drug dealer, a terrorist, or a tax evader. Actually, the morality involved in all those activities is worth a separate discussion... it's perverse they're always classed together.

But this is what we can look forward to.

Now, that doesn't mean that bitcoin won't still be valuable. That's because, as I've said before, three-quarters of the people on earth live in the Third World. These people use currencies that are worth little within their own countries. Outside of their country, they're worth nothing. They're "blocked" currencies. So, these people will continue to use bitcoin, or other cryptos, to a growing degree. There's trouble brewing.

And let me add something else. I've said for some time that bitcoin is a wonderful thing. But what happens when somebody develops bitcoin 2.0? I'm talking about a digital currency that uses a considerably better or different technology. What happens then to the value of bitcoin? It will likely collapse.

But these aren't even the main reasons to be concerned about bitcoin.

Justin: So, what would be?

Doug: The development of quantum computing power poses a huge threat to bitcoin.

The little computers that are making bitcoin today will be obviated.

Now, I don't know when quantum computing will be become commercial or practical—although it seems quite soon. But when it does, no code will be uncrackable. So any alteration of blockchain may be possible. Who knows? It's been said that any sufficiently advanced technology is indistinguishable from magic.

But, entirely apart from that, the owners of quantum devices will be able to create bitcoin or its look-alikes in gigantic quantities almost instantly. Of course, at that point we're living in the world of the Singularity—and the price of bitcoin will be the least of our worries. Or opportunities.

There are all kinds of X-factors that most people haven't considered.

But there's the biggest one. Cryptos have gone hyperbolic. At $18,000 a Bitcoin, I no longer have the nerve to play the game. After all, it's gone up about 18,000% this year. I'm happy to leave something on the table for the next guy.

Justin: What about governments that are trying to launch their own digital currencies?

Doug: A certainty. And it's happening as we speak. We're living in the digital age. Everybody has a smartphone today. And governments are developing their own digital currencies to take advantage of that fact…

In the U.S., they'll call it FedCoin. In Japan, it will be called JCoin or something. The Russians will come up with their own digital currency too.

Even the Venezuelans are trying to go digital with Petrocoin. Of course, they'll fail miserably. That's because digital currencies only work if there's an element of trust. And there's zero trust with them. But there should be zero trust with any government.

Still, governments around the world will try this because they want to eliminate paper currency completely.

Justin: And why do they want to do that?

Doug: They want to herd everyone into the digital money system. That way they can know absolutely everything about your entire financial life.

They'll know what you buy… what you sell… how much you earn… and how much money you've tucked away. Everything.

Not only that, they'll be able to confiscate everything that you own at will if everything is digital and online—if you use their digital currency.

So, this is a big deal.

Justin: Do you think the average person will go along with this? Or will the "War on Cash" push more people into bitcoin?

Doug: Worse. The average person will not just go along with the government's plans, but support them enthusiastically.

The average person trusts authorities. They trust the government. They buy into the nonsense about "We the People" and such.

Plus, it's convenient to do everything digitally. And the average person values convenience much more than privacy—which no longer exists anyway. Many people prefer it this way.

In China, for instance, millions of people are already involved in China's social credit system. Everything they do, everything about them, is online. Your credit score… where you live… what kind of job you have… your habits… your thoughts… your friends. And everything about your friends too.

You get a social credit rating. And if you're a "good citizen," you'll get the equivalent of frequent-flyer points for associating with the right people, putting out the right memes, doing as you're told, and so forth. If you don't, you're overtly and also subtlety punished. So people will vie with each other to show they have Orwellian Goodthink.

It makes me feel like a dinosaur who sees a big asteroid about to hit the Earth. People with individualism and personal freedom as central values won't do well in the near future. Neither will Western Civilization.

This is all part of a much larger trend. The world is basically turning into something of a hive. And as far as I'm concerned, it's another reason to privately buy small gold coins and put them aside. I expect other countries to follow China's lead, certainly including the US.

Justin: It sounds like you've turned bearish on bitcoin.

Doug: Well, as I've said before, I was first exposed to bitcoin when somebody gave me one in 2013. It was worth $13 at the time, and I still have the physical token.

And last summer, I bought a bunch of bitcoin and other cryptocurrencies.

Since then, I've more than quadrupled my money. But the market is getting too bubbly for me. It's a lot like junior mining stocks after the public gets involved. It's not the time to buy. It's the time to sell. And, incidentally, buy small mining stocks—they're now extremely cheap. But nobody cares. Which is typical of a bottom.

Justin: So, have you sold all your bitcoin? Or are you just no longer a buyer?

Doug: I'm a firm believer that you should make the trend your friend. This is because a trend in motion tends to stay in motion until a serious event or crisis breaks the trend.

Based on that, I'm inclined to hold, certainly at least until January 1—hardly forever. So, I don't have to pay taxes on my gains this year.

I don't know how high bitcoin will go. Some smart people think it could go as high $30,000. Or $1 million. These aren't stupid people, either.

Justin: Doug, your network includes some of the world's top cryptocurrency experts like John McAfee.

What are these guys saying these days?

Doug: I haven't talked to John about bitcoin since it hit $20,000.

But he still thinks that it's going to hit $1 million.

I'll have a chance to explore his reasoning when I visit the Solomon Islands with him in February. That's another, and somewhat exotic, story.

But I'm skeptical of that price target, however, because there will someday be 21 million bitcoins, according to the bitcoin protocol. There are about 16.7 million out now—although a good number have apparently been permanently lost.

Anyway, if you multiply 21 million by $1 million, you get $21 trillion. That's more than the annual economic output (GDP) of the entire U.S. economy. That's a bit outlandish. On the other hand, if every millionaire in the world—it's said there are around 20 million—were to own just one...

I've heard the pros and cons. There's reason to be skeptical of the market. You could have tried to pick a top at $10, $100, $500, or even $1,000 and you would have been made a fool. I'm playing higher prices via the shares of a couple of bitcoin miners—the bubble has yet to really expand in the stock market.

It's very hard to call tops during a mania. But the money is now very big and serious. One thing is for sure, it's not the time to be buying more bitcoin.

Of course, bitcoin could soar to $100,000 and make a liar out of me. I hope it does—if only because the big payers are mostly libertarians. And I like having rich libertarian friends. But I doubt it.

Justin: Only time will tell. Anyway, thanks again for taking the time to speak with me.

Doug: My pleasure, Justin.

Doug Casey on the World's Biggest Revolution

ORIGINALLY PUBLISHED ON SEPTEMBER 5, 2017

Justin's note: South Korea just made history. It just introduced a "robot tax." It became the first country to adopt this policy. Now, to be fair, this isn't a tax at all. But it will make it more expensive for South Korean companies to invest in technology. Under the current law, South Korean companies can deduct up to 7% of how much money they spend on automation equipment or robots. But soon they'll only be able to deduct 2% of their investment. The government hopes this will encourage companies to hire workers instead of buying robots…

Justin: Doug, what do you make of this robot tax? Should governments be discouraging companies from investing in innovation?

Doug: It's incredibly stupid. I'm especially surprised to see the South Koreans be the ones to take the first step in this direction.

South Korea is one of the most technologically advanced countries in the world. It's much more advanced on a per-capita basis than the United States or any place in Europe. Most of the countries in East Asia—most prominently Singapore, Hong Kong, Taiwan, Japan, South Korea, and most recently China—have been advancing at warp speed for decades. That's partially because of their social ethos, but mainly because they're very low-tax, low-regulation jurisdictions—like the US was during its golden age.

So, it's very disturbing to see the South Koreans moving in this direction.

Justin: Why would they do this? And do you think other countries will follow suit?

Doug: Why indeed? The reasons offered have to do with preventing unemployment, heading off social unrest, and garnering more tax revenue. The real reasons however, in my view, are fear of the unknown and ignorance of economics.

There's been a lot of talk about taxing robots. The meme is gaining traction with both the talking heads and the *hoi polloi*. Bill Gates is a big proponent, which further cements his status as being an idiot savant.

What he wants to do is to not just withdraw the tax benefits for investing in robotic technology, but actually tax robots the way that a human worker would be taxed.

The rationale behind this is that since robots could replace from 15 to 35% of all human jobs within the next 10 years, something must be done to slow that trend. And generate tax revenue to put those newly unemployed people on welfare or whatnot.

These people want to slow down the rise of the robots. And taxes will certainly do that by discouraging businesses from investing in them. But what's even worse, Gates wants to use the income from the tax on robots to increase welfare benefits for the unemployed. Which is especially stupid, because you get the things that you encourage. And when you pay people for not working, or you make it possible for them to not work, that's exactly what they're going to do.

So, it's a very, very bad trend, promoted by Gates, and implemented by the South Koreans.

Justin: Should the government do anything to prevent robots from taking people's jobs?

Doug: No, there's absolutely nothing that the government should be doing about this.

What would have happened if government had decided to do something about the rise of the cotton gin during the first Industrial Revolution? Or mechanical weaving machines, which unemployed millions of "cottage industry" spinners and weavers working with primitive foot-powered looms in their shacks? The Bessemer furnace, the steam engine, the railroad, and a thousand other technologies in the first industrial revolution?

In those days, technophobes were known as Luddites; they wanted to destroy the new machines in order to save their unproductive jobs. If they'd succeeded, we'd all still be primitive benighted peasants.

Any government interference withdraws capital from productive areas of the economy, and redirects it to some politically favored parts of the economy. Robots and artificial intelligence (AI) are the friend of the average man; they catapult the average standard of living much higher.

Justin: So, you're saying the government should just get out of the way?

Doug: The government should withdraw itself not just from robots and artificial intelligence (AI), but from the economy in general. The State is, by its nature, a coercive institution. And coercion of any type should be kept to a minimum in any society. That means the State should be limited to protecting you from domestic coercion with police. Foreign coercion with an army. And facilitating the adjudication of disputes with a court system. In today's world, however, it does none of those things effectively—but tries to do everything else.

I find it most disturbing that even in today's world, when much more is known about economics than ever, that people still look at government, which is a coercive force, as something that should involve itself in the economy. It's very discouraging.

Justin: So, what should people do if the government stays out of this? How can they prepare for the robotics age?

Doug: There's no question that robots and AI are going to hugely expand. Their power is increasing at the rate of Moore's Law. In other words, the power of computing is doubling roughly every 18 to 24 months, while the cost halves. This is also true in the areas of biotech, nanotech, and genetic engineering. These technologies are going to fundamentally transform the very nature of life itself.

In a decade or two, robots will be more intelligent, more innovative, and perhaps even more thoughtful than humans. They're not just going to be the odd-looking mechanical beast that can perform a few parlor tricks like today. Soon, there will be not just mechanical robots, but biological robots. Who knows what will come after that.

We're really on the cusp of the biggest revolution in world history. I look forward to it. It will cure disease and old age. The avalanche of new wealth that will be created will effectively eliminate poverty. Mankind's wildest dreams and ambitions can be realized. People who are trying to slow this process down are worse than stupid—they're criminal.

So, what should you do about it?

The first thing you have to remember is that there's no need for unemployment in the world. Everybody—myself, you, and all the other seven billion people in the world—have an unlimited desire for goods and services.

So, theoretically, anybody could be able to work 24 hours a day, seven days a week, providing goods and services that other people want. The presence of robots will just make that easier, more efficient and more profitable.

And there are always going to be things that people can do better than robots. Point number one. So, there's no need to be unemployed.

Justin: What's the other reason?

Doug: Point number two is that the intelligence of computers and robots is increasing exponentially.

This will liberate people to do things—most of which we haven't even thought of yet—that they'll still be able to do better than machines. Years ago, IBM came up with the slogan "Machines should work, people should think." The world is moving towards that ideal at the speed of Moore's Law—as long as government, and busybodies like Gates, don't slow down progress.

Not so long ago you were working 12 hours a day, loading 16 tons of coal in an underground coal mine, just to keep body and soul together; by the time you got home, you were just too tired and didn't have time to do any creative, productive work. Unless the trend indicated by Bill Gates and the South Koreans continues, in a generation we'll think of today's world as being almost as oppressive and backward. Much of the work we do today is "dog work." Good riddance to it.

I believe the trend to robotics and AI is a very favorable thing from both a humanist and a spiritual point of view. It's immensely favorable from an economic point of view as well.

The problem—if there is one—is that government will try to use these robots to control the populace. And the military will be the biggest user of these things everywhere.

So, it's very dangerous. The movie The Terminator will be much more predictive than previously imagined.

Justin: That's certainly a threat to consider. But what about the opportunity here? Have you personally invested in any robotics or AI companies?

Doug: No, I haven't, because although most of the reading that I do is about either science or history, and I've got a reasonable theoretical grip on these things, I don't feel like I have enough personal tactical competence in these areas to decide which company's going to be a winner. It's something I might look into more, exactly which companies are actively involved in these areas. Because it might be an excellent place to place some bets. Everybody wants to find the next Apple, Google, or Microsoft.

Justin: Absolutely. A lot of money is going to be made in that space. So, let us know if you find any investments. Thanks for taking the time to speak with me today, Doug.

Doug: My pleasure.

Doug Casey on Asset Seizures

───

ORIGINALLY PUBLISHED ON AUGUST 21, 2017

Justin's note: Jeff Sessions wants to steal your property. Sessions is the U.S. Attorney General. Since taking office, he's done all sorts of idiotic things. He's threatened to crack down on the legal marijuana market. He's attacked gay rights. And now, he wants to amp up asset seizures…

Justin: Doug, what do you think of Sessions' latest "bright" idea?

Doug: Well, let me preface this by saying Sessions was a disastrous choice for Attorney General. He's done nothing in his life but be a lawyer, a prosecutor, and a politician. He has no experience—and therefore probably no inclination or even ability—to produce things of tangible value.

But we almost always get undesirables as the AG. They're hatchet men, meant to prosecute "the enemy," taking their pick of the hundreds of thousands of laws and regulations on the books to do so. Look at some of the recent AGs—Loretta Lynch, Eric Holder, Alberto Gonzales, John Ashcroft, Janet Reno. All of them would have been willing and obedient lapdogs to Stalin or Beria. A certain personality type is suited for the job.

Sessions is a rabid drug warrior, even against something as useful and benign as hemp, or marijuana. He's a busybody who feels no guilt or remorse at enforcing laws that have destroyed the lives of tens of millions. I don't know if he's stupid, bent, thoughtless, paranoid or what his problem might be. Maybe he's afraid that if pot wasn't illegal he'd become a dope fiend himself. But the proper direction, the objective, is to legalize all drugs. Not amp the drug war up another notch, as he wants to do.

And not only does he want to amp up the drug war, but he wants to increase the State's ability to confiscate citizens' property—especially cash—on even suspicion of breaking a law.

In the meantime he's not doing anything to investigate the people in Hillary's camp for all kinds of apparent illegality. In fact, now that Trump's in office, what ever happened to his promise of a real investigation of what really happened to things like Building 7 on 9/11? Or the strange deaths that seem to have surrounded the Clinton clan for decades?

So far the man seems all negatives no positives. He's just another Deep State actor who's climbed the political ladder a little higher. These guys all protect each other.

But increasingly many of Trump's choices are disastrous, like his National Security Advisor McMaster and White House Chief of Staff Kelly. And wormtongues Ivanka and Jared Kushner. This is perhaps an inevitable problem when a President is just a pragmatist with no philosophical core. Although, I hasten to add, having no core may be better than having a rotten core, like Obama and others in the recent past.

Justin: Not to mention, asset seizures don't work. Over the past decade, the federal government has seized more than $28 billion. But that's done absolutely nothing to deter crime.

So, why would Sessions double down on this failed policy? Is he clueless? Or is the government just that desperate?

Doug: Good question. Well, I've already speculated on some possible aspects of Session's character that might partially explain this. But all the repressive aspects of government—civil forfeitures are just one—have been growing and compounding for years. It's not a conspiracy, it's the natural progression of all living organisms. They all want to grow, exert more control on their environments, and become more powerful. The problem is that government has unusual powers, and no longer seems to have many limits. So you can expect this trend to accelerate.

I saw the other day the government steals more from the American people through confiscations than is lost outright to robberies and muggings. It's been reported that in 2015 civil forfeitures exceeded the amount stolen by all robbers. It's quite amazing and disturbing. There are at least two reasons things are deteriorating.

Number one, as a general rule, police are no longer trained as "peace officers." They're trained to be, and view themselves, as "law enforcement officers." This is a very different thing. The police are a bigger threat to your property and your liberty, not to mention your life, than actual criminals. Number two, these governments are all bankrupt. They're looking for revenue wherever they can get it. Predators are most dangerous when they're hungry.

The police are the ones that actually make it happen, and they have a vested interest in doing the wrong thing. Whenever a police department confiscates things under these laws, they get to keep some percentage. It varies, but can be 10, 20, 30, 50 percent of what's confiscated, and they love it because the money goes to the local police department in question. They can use it for buying fun cop toys, or for buying further educational benefits, or whatever, for themselves. So, they're profiting from this stuff as directly as the criminals do that steal things from citizens. It's a total disaster.

And remember, the Attorney General is the country's top law enforcement officer.

Justin: Yeah, it's scary.

Unfortunately, the government is sinking deeper in debt by the day. So, I'm afraid this is going to get worse before it gets better. Do you agree?

Doug: It's inevitable.

These governments are digging themselves into deep financial holes. They're going to need more and more revenue. The populace has been trained to see the government as a cornucopia. As the economy goes into the trailing edge of the current financial hurricane, they're going to demand even more freebies from all levels of government. So, the trend will continue until there's some type of a crisis. At which point anything can happen.

The downtrend is in motion. And trends in motion tend to continue and accelerate until they change. I like to draw attention to France in 1789, a horrible situation with its highly authoritarian and totally bankrupt government. A revolution was necessary and welcome. But then things got worse under Robespierre. And worse again under Napoleon. The exact same thing with Russia in 1917—but then they got Lenin, and then Stalin.

Justin: Absolutely. So, asset seizures won't even put a dent in the government's debt problem.

With that said, how else might the government steal money and property from people?

Doug: Well, they're now talking about making you declare your cryptocurrencies whenever you cross a border. If you don't, and they find out, they're eligible for confiscation. As cryptocurrencies get bigger—and they will—this will constitute both a gigantic invasion of privacy and an attack on your wealth.

All governments already ask whether you have more than $10,000 when you cross their borders, and reserve the right to search you. If this becomes law, it means that you, your computer, and your smartphone will always be liable to a full forensic audit.

It's another major step towards the world of 1984. Every new law they pass has Kafka-esque possibilities. That's what legislatures around the world do every day they're in session. All of these laws have severe penalties. The trend in this direction—which started in earnest just over 100 years ago—is going hyperbolic. And the average human—miseducated, propagandized, and besotted by food and drugs—wants more laws. Why? I think fear is today's dominant emotional tone. People want to be protected and cared for, like farm animals. They see the State as their benevolent shepherd.

There are no positive political trends in today's world. They aren't cutting back on regulations, reducing taxes, or eliminating laws anywhere. They're doing just the opposite.

Justin: So, how can people protect themselves from this?

Doug: It's increasingly hard because the statists, collectivists, socialists, fascists, globalists, and the like have won the war for the hearts and minds of the masses all over the world. And the world's governments—notwithstanding their inevitable wars and such—are cooperating with each other far, far more than ever before.

In a nutshell, there are three things to keep in mind.

First, become as wealthy as possible. Although they can steal anything and everything from you, the more you have the more damage you can sustain, and the more influence you can exert.

Second, diversify politically and geographically. You want to have some convenient options if your government starts looking like Russia in the '20s, or Germany in the '30s, China in the '50s, Cuba in the '60s, etc., etc. It's a very long list.

Third, keep your head down. The tall poppy is the one selected for cutting. I observe my first two rules, but not so much this one. That's because sometimes we have to make a choice between what's smart and what's right. In my case, almost nothing is worth feeling like a whipped dog.

Justin: Thanks for taking the time to speak with me today, Doug.

Doug: My pleasure.

Doug Casey on Genderless Babies

———

ORIGINALLY PUBLISHED ON AUGUST 14, 2017

Justin's note: Just when I thought I'd seen it all… I recently read a story about a baby born in Canada that wasn't designated a sex. Its birth certificate simply lists "U" under the sex category. The Gender Free ID Coalition believes that this stands for "unspecified or unknown." But it's impossible to know for sure. You see, this has never happened before. It's a "world first," according to CNN…

Justin: What do you make of this, Doug?

Doug: The parent in question is obviously very confused. Perhaps they've just been brainwashed by the wave of political correctness that's washed over the world like a tsunami of raw sewage; if so, it's possible they can recover. Perhaps they have the neurological wiring of one sex but the body of the other; I imagine that's quite possible, and is nobody's "fault." Maybe they experienced some childhood trauma that made them hate their own sex, or gender, or whatever. Maybe any of a number of other things.

In times past, someone like this would be viewed as a curiosity. They might have worked in a circus sideshow. Today they're taken seriously.

Look, almost everybody has problems, fears, inadequacies—issues—of one type or another. But if you want to succeed, you do your best trying to overcome, de-emphasize, or hide these things. You don't go out in public and broadcast them. Why not? For the same reason a chicken with a physical peculiarity doesn't—the rest of the flock will peck her to death. This person isn't courageous; he's just got less sense than a chicken.

What's worse, this person is burdening a child with their psychological aberrations—not very nice on the part of the parent. I'm a believer in nature over nurture, so the kid will likely survive and be whoever he/she or it is. But the idiot parent isn't going to make growing up any easier for him, her, or it. Then again, I understand Facebook has designated about 48 sexual or gender identities… And people seem to live on Facebook.

I take a scientific view on these things. Unless you're born a hermaphrodite, you're equipped as either a male or a female, with designated X and Y chromosomes. If the kid wants a sex change later in life—and can afford to pay for it—then that should be a possibility. But for the parent to put that on its birth certificate is nothing but a political statement.

As far as I'm concerned, you can call yourself whatever you want. If a person wants to self-identify as a two-headed crustacean from Mars, that's fine. Anybody should be or do or have whatever they want—as long as they don't aggress against other people or their property.

I mean who cares how you "self-identify"? You're giving other people more information by which they can judge what type of a being you are.

I like more information about the person I'm dealing with. I think the current trend to self-identify as all manner of bizarre things is aberrant, and even sick. But it's a matter of personal choice. The key is not getting the State or the law involved.

Justin: So, what's fueling this trend?

Doug: This is just one of the many subsets of a greater phenomenon: the collapse of Western Civilization.

Western Civilization is built upon the acknowledgment and understanding of physical reality, and concepts such as truth, honesty, and science. When Bizzarro World is accepted as being equally valid in the eyes of the law and most people, then a society is in trouble.

This whole multi-gender, sex change and whatever trend is just one subset of the worms eating away at the culture. It's why primitive and authoritarian forces like Islam are on the rise. They're retrogressive, and repugnant to anyone that believes in Western values. But they offer certainty about what's right and wrong, proper and improper. And—sad to say—the average person may be so degraded that he'll choose that over the uncertainty presented by personal freedom and responsibility. It's a pity. Many, or even most, of the people in the West are renouncing personal freedom and responsibility—even denying the reality of being born a boy or a girl—and substituting them with floating abstractions.

Justin: What role should the government play in all this? Should they acknowledge these things?

Doug: Well frankly, I don't believe in government identification documents, driver's licenses, or anything of the sort. Yes, I understand that over the last 100 years society has come to accept the supposed "necessity" of everyone having "papers," like a dog or a cow. It's a very recent phenomenon. But insofar as ID is needed, the market could and would provide it far better than the State. Are you a non-person if you don't have a birth certificate?

If this whole intersex, transgender thing wasn't politicized it would be a non-problem. People have always thought and believed things that are not just outlandish but at odds with reality. But frankly, who cares—as long as they can't impose their views on anyone else? They're destroying their own lives, but it's not my problem. Although it's a symptom of a much bigger problem.

But, to answer your question directly, the doctor should put "male" or "female" in the box, because those are the choices that correspond with physical reality at the time.

Justin: I agree, Doug. The state should leave this alone.

But I will say that it's hard to stay on top of all the developments in the gender world. Just look at this survey that VIDA, a non-profit feminist organization, put out recently (image on page 86):

There are 26 "sub-genders" to choose from. I didn't even know that was a thing until I saw this.

Doug: Yeah, they're really innovative. Insane, actually. I'd say they hate themselves even more than I'm sure they hate straight white males.

There are clearly many flavors of psychological aberration. Once again, it's nothing that the politicians should get involved in. Let people put down whatever they want on their survey cards.

I just feel sorry for the kids of these crazy people. It's going to make their lives harder, but not everybody is dealt a Royal Flush at birth. On the bright side, maybe Nietzsche was right when he said "That which does not kill us makes us stronger."

So, here's a kid that's going to start playing his game of Texas Hold 'Em of life with an unsuited 2-7. I'm sorry for him, but that's what we call the luck of the draw. He's going to grow up likely having to endure all kinds of harassment. A bit like what Johnny Cash sang about in "A Boy Named Sue."

VIDA Women in Literary Arts

The 2016 VIDA Count Intersectional Survey (continued)

Gender (continued)

2. Please check or fill-in all that apply:

☐ Transgender		☐ Genderqueer	
☐ Cisgender		☐ Hijra (Indian/South Asian)	
☐ Agender		☐ Intersex	
☐ Bigender		☐ Mahu (Native Hawaiian)	
☐ Binary		☐ Multiply-gendered or Multigender	
☐ Butch		☐ Nonbinary	
☐ Coercively assigned female at birth (CAFAB)		☐ Polygender	
☐ Coercively assigned male at birth (CAMAB)		☐ Trans+	
☐ Demigirl/Demiwoman		☐ Transfeminine	
☐ Demiboy/Demiman		☐ Transmasculine	
☐ Fa'afafine (Samoan)		☐ Transmisogyny constrained (TMC)	
☐ Femme		☐ Two Spirit (Native American, First Nation)	
☐ Genderfluid		☐ Decline to state	
☐ Gender non-conforming			

A gender identity not listed. Please share how you identify:

☐

Justin: But what about the child? They obviously had zero say in this. Should the government prevent people with "psychological aberrations" from doing this to children?

Doug: Well, you and I may think that these people have psychological problems. But who can objectively quantify this?

It would likely be left up to psychiatrists. But my experience is that psychiatry is the lowest rung of specialties on the medical ladder. They generally don't have to know any real medicine beyond what it took to get their union card. Their cure for psychological problems is generally passing out pills, many of which are extremely dangerous. Plus, most psychiatrists are troubled people themselves. They become psychiatrists to bounce their own aberrations off of the person that's paying them there to tell them his.

They're the last people to make this determination.

We can all have our opinions on who's crazy. But I don't think there should be any formalized law or regulation on the topic.

I don't want the state involved in any of this stuff.

You know, in Germany there are some names that you can't give your kid. They won't allow you to call your kid "Freedom" or "Liberty." Those names are illegal to give your kid in Germany. Freedom isn't much in fashion in the land of Karl Marx, National Socialism, the Stasi, Christian Democracy, Social Democracy, and what-have-you.

Then again, why shouldn't some state bureaucrat determine what I call my kid, or for that matter what the kid calls himself? God forbid the drones and proles might get the idea they could actually own themselves!

Justin: Thanks for taking the time to speak with me today, Doug.

Doug: My pleasure.

Doug Casey on "Offensive" Words

ORIGINALLY PUBLISHED ON AUGUST 4, 2017

Justin's note: Stop saying offensive words. That's what the Associated Press (AP) is telling writers. You see, the AP puts out a stylebook every year that includes universal guidelines for stylistic matters like punctuation, capitalization, and even word choice. In this year's version, the AP encouraged writers to not use words such as "pro-life," "migrant," "refugee," "Islamist," and "terrorist." It's completely ludicrous. Yet, sadly, it's a sign of the times…

Justin: Doug, what do you think of the AP censoring writers? Are you surprised at all?

Doug: There was once a time when journalists often had intelligence, integrity, and competence. Many did their jobs—reporting the news accurately, openly disclosing their bias (if any). H.L. Mencken was a model of what a journalist should be. He wasn't just a reporter. He was a literary maven who had immense stores of knowledge and well-thought-out, fact-based opinions on nearly everything. In addition to a myriad of newspaper and magazine articles, he even wrote a definitive book on the English language and the correct way to use it.

Today, reporters have none of these qualifications. Their only qualification appears to be a BA degree in English, or Journalism.

Maybe it's just that giants walked the earth in the days before Political Correctness. If Mencken was alive today, he would be shocked and appalled at the midgets who pass for reporters and editors today. He'd be rolling in laughter and disgust at how much the profession has been degraded.

It's like Orwell's worst nightmare is coming true. In his novel *Nineteen Eighty-Four*, the idea behind "doublethink" is to alter the nature of language. Big Brother wants to reduce the number of words that exist, eliminating those that describe non-PC thoughts and actions. They seem to want to institute Newspeak—complete with thoughtcrime, goodthink, bellyfeel, and prolefeed.

Justin: And why is that such a big deal?

Doug: Words enable thought. So if you corrupt words, you can alter and corrupt people's thoughts. Words are the parents of thought. And thought is the father to action. There's a reason the Bible speaks of "the word" with such respect.

If you don't have a word for something, it makes it hard to think about it. And it's worse if you have the wrong word. They're trying to corrupt the language to limit what people think and do.

Justin: Why are they trying to alter how people think?

Doug: They say it's to help make people "better." Of course their idea of what's good, and my idea of what's good differ radically. The Nazis and Soviets tried to make people "better" by using propaganda—propaganda is actually fake news. They say they're trying to reduce friction in society, or make the "underprivileged" feel good about themselves. But in fact they're doing the opposite. They're quite happy to use the violence of the State to enforce their views on society.

The people doing this are worms. They're acting to destroy civilization and civil society. These people are the intellectual equivalent of the thugs that pour into the streets to commit arson and looting.

They can't be so stupid as to think that if they ban impolite words for certain racial and ethnic groups, that will actually ban hostile feelings. It probably does just the opposite. It's like tightening down the lid on a pressure cooker when you don't allow people to express themselves.

A lot of these AP words seem to carry racial connotations. Something it's apparently non-PC to acknowledge.

Oddly, it's only whites, males, and Christians that have to be careful using "hate speech" or non-PC speech today. Members of so-called "historically oppressed" minorities can say whatever they want. Which is pretty rich, since they're actually majorities in many parts of the US today. And their native cultures allow for about zero freedom of speech—or any other kind of freedom, for that matter.

Actually, people ought to express themselves in any politically incorrect words they wish. Any words they choose to use.

Justin: And why's that?

Doug: Because then you can find out what a person's really thinking. You can find out what kind of a person you're dealing with. You can judge if it's a good person or a bad person based on how he may characterize or not characterize other people. If you limit other people's freedom of speech, you're really just limiting your own ability to get information—not just from them, but *about* them.

It's shameful that the AP is telling journalists what they can and can't say to influence what the readers are able to think. And equally shameful that there's no protest from the reporters.

It's not just the AP. When you read something in *The New York Times*, *The Washington Post*, or practically any establishment mouthpiece today you can rely on lots of confused, conflated and intentionally misleading weasel words. I wrote an essay on this last September. I urge readers to take a look at it for a laundry list of them[1].

Justin: I remember that essay, Doug. In it, you discussed how many of the words we hear on television and other media are confused, conflated, or completely misused.

You went down a long list of words, including inflation, money, and justice.

Could we do the same thing with a few of the words that the AP blacklisted? Let's start with "pro-life." Should writers really say "anti-abortion" instead?

Doug: Well, the term "pro-life" expresses a certain moral stance, with implied political preferences. It's a favorable towards giving birth to babies. It has that connotation.

"Anti-abortion," however, means exactly the same thing. But it's better rhetorical technique to be "pro" than "anti"—to be for something than against something. The other side says they're "pro-choice."

In fact, in a neutral context, one that has nothing to do with babies and abortion, most people of good will are both "pro-choice" and "pro-life." Who would be "anti-life" or "anti-choice"?

It's all about influencing the hoi polloi by using words cleverly. If the argument was conducted on strictly intellectual grounds—which it's not, it's conducted on mostly emotional grounds—the proper words would be neutral. But they don't want people to think, they want them to feel.

The whole subject is intellectually dishonest. Both sides attempt appealing to emotion and the psychological aberrations of the listeners, not cool reason.

---

1. www.internationalman.com/articles/doug-casey-on-the-recent-corruptions-of-the-english-language

Justin: Sounds like these guidelines only make things more confusing. Is that the point?

Doug: Correct, the whole objective is to confuse, muddy, and befuddle thoughts.

For example, they say you're not supposed to use the word "migrant" but that's exactly what these people are. I guess you're also supposed to call them "refugees", whether or not they are. Most are actually economic opportunity seekers. There's nothing wrong with that, but it's not as sympathetic.

They're not "immigrants." An immigrant is somebody that formally enters the country by the recipients' rules and norms. That's what an immigrant is. He's completely legal.

A migrant might be somebody that comes across as part of an invading horde, legality has nothing to do with it. That's the connotation but it's an accurate one. It's exactly what these people are. If there are enough of them, and they're armed, you can reclassify them from "migrant" to "invader."

They're an informal and unarmed invading army of a totally different culture, race, religion, and language. So of course, they are migrants.

It's too bad that it's too un-PC to call them what they are. I really believe you've got to call a spade a spade. Tough luck if some cupcake thinks it's a microaggression impinging on his safe space.

We haven't talked about another word on the list, "Islamist". That's a good one. Let's save it for another day.

Justin: "Terrorist" was another word on the AP's blacklist. Instead of saying that, it encourages writers to say "militant," "attacker," or "lone wolf."

Doug: Terrorist. I find that interesting. You're not supposed to call somebody a terrorist. Does that mean only the government can designate somebody as a terrorist?

Anyway, terrorist is a word that's used improperly. It turns out there are roughly 125 definitions of the word terrorist, different official definitions used by various government agencies at one time or another. To me, terrorism is simply a method of warfare. It's a tactic, like artillery barrages or cavalry charges. It's a legitimate method of warfare.

Now, whether somebody's actually a terrorist or not is a different question. Is he part of an organized military, a paramilitary group, or a revolutionary group? The word is a pejorative. But can a terrorist ever be a good guy? Were Allied bomber crews conducting terror raids on German cities in World War 2 bad guys?

These things have to be discussed, not just glossed over. I'll offer a definition of terrorism. It's "an act of wholesale violence, for political ends, that deliberately targets civilians." Most terrorism in the world has always been conducted by legitimate States.

It's all completely insane. But this is what's characterizing today's society. How something is phrased has a huge impact on how the public thinks about it. It's why I'm a Freedom Fighter, you're a Rebel, but he's a Terrorist.

Anyway, two years from now my novel, *Terrorist* is going to be out where I'm going to go into this in a lot of detail.

Justin: Thanks for taking the time to speak with me today, Doug. I'm looking forward to the new book.

Doug: My pleasure, Justin.

Doug Casey on the Coming Financial Crisis

—

ORIGINALLY PUBLISHED ON JULY 14, 2017

Justin's note: We won't have another financial crisis "in our lifetimes." It's a crazy idea. After all, it feels like the U.S. is long overdue for a major crisis. But that's what Janet Yellen thinks. The Fed chair said: Would I say there will never, ever be another financial crisis? [...] Probably that would be going too far. But I do think we're much safer, and I hope that it will not be in our lifetimes, and I don't believe it will be. I couldn't believe my eyes when I read this...

Justin: Doug, I know you disagree with Yellen. But I'm wondering why she would even say this? Has she lost her mind?

Doug: Listening to the silly woman say that made me think we're truly living in Bizarro World. It's identical in tone to what stock junkies said in 1999 just before the tech bubble burst. She's going to go down in history as the modern equivalent of Irving Fisher, who said "we've reached a permanent plateau of prosperity," in 1929, just before the Great Depression started.

I don't care that some university gave her a Ph.D., and some politicians made her Fed Chair, possibly the second most powerful person in the world. She's ignorant of economics, ignorant of history, and clearly has no judgment about what she says for the record.

Why would she say such a thing? I guess because since she really believes throwing trillions of dollars at the banking system will create prosperity. It started with the $750 billion bailout at the beginning of the last crisis. They've since thrown another $4 trillion at the financial system.

All of that money has flowed into the banking system. So, the banking system has a lot of liquidity at the moment, and she thinks that means the economy is going to be fine.

Justin: Hasn't all that liquidity made the banking system safer?

Doug: No. The whole banking system is screwed-up and unstable. It's a gigantic accident waiting to happen.

People forgot that we now have a fractional reserve banking system. It's very different from a classical banking system. I suspect not one person in 1,000 understands the difference…

Modern banking emerged from the goldsmithing trade of the Middle Ages. Being a goldsmith required a working inventory of precious metal, and managing that inventory profitably required expertise in buying and selling metal and storing it securely. Those capacities segued easily into the business of lending and borrowing gold, which is to say the business of lending and borrowing money.

Most people today are only dimly aware that until the early 1930s, gold coins were used in everyday commerce by the general public. In addition, gold backed most national currencies at a fixed rate of convertibility. Banks were just another business—nothing special. They were distinguished from other enterprises only by the fact they stored, lent, and borrowed gold coins, not as a sideline but as a primary business. Bankers had become goldsmiths without the hammers.

Bank deposits, until quite recently, fell strictly into two classes, depending on the preference of the depositor and the terms offered by banks: time deposits, and demand deposits. Although the distinction between them has been lost in recent years, respecting the difference is a critical element of sound banking practice.

Justin: Can you explain the difference between a time deposit and demand deposit?

Doug: Sure. With a time deposit—a savings account, in essence—a customer contracts to leave his money with the banker for a specified period. In return, he receives a specified fee (interest) for his risk, for his inconvenience, and as consideration for allowing the banker the use of the depositor's money. The banker, secure in knowing he has a specific amount of gold for a specific amount of time, is able to lend it; he'll do so at an interest rate high enough to cover expenses (including the interest promised to the depositor), fund a loan-loss reserve, and if all goes according to plan, make a profit.

A time deposit entails a commitment by both parties. The depositor is locked in until the due date. How could a sound banker promise to give a time depositor his money back on demand and without penalty when he's planning to lend it out?

In the business of accepting time deposits, a banker is a dealer in credit, acting as an intermediary between lenders and borrowers. To avoid loss, bankers customarily preferred to lend on productive assets, whose earnings offered assurance that the borrower could cover the interest as it came due. And they were willing to lend only a fraction of the value of a pledged asset, to ensure a margin of safety for the principal. And only for a limited time—such as against the harvest of a crop or the sale of an inventory. And finally, only to people of known good character—the first line of defense against fraud. Long-term loans were the province of bond syndicators.

That's time deposits.

Justin: And what about demand deposits?

Doug: Demand deposits were a completely different matter.

Demand deposits were so called because, unlike time deposits, they were payable to the customer on demand. These are the basis of checking accounts. The banker doesn't pay interest on the money, because he supposedly never has the use of it; to the contrary, he necessarily charged the depositor a fee for:

1. Assuming the responsibility of keeping the money safe, available for immediate withdrawal, and…

2. Administering the transfer of the money if the depositor so chooses, by either writing a check or passing along a warehouse receipt that represents the gold on deposit.

An honest banker should no more lend out demand deposit money than Allied Van and Storage should lend out the furniture you've paid it to store. The warehouse receipts for gold were called banknotes. When a government issued them, they were called currency. Gold bullion, gold coinage, banknotes, and currency together constituted the society's supply of transaction media. But its amount was strictly limited by the amount of gold actually available to people.

Sound principles of banking are identical to sound principles of warehousing any kind of merchandise—whether it's autos, potatoes, or books. Or money. There's nothing mysterious about sound banking. But banking all over the world has been fundamentally unsound since government-sponsored central banks came to dominate the financial system.

Central banks are a linchpin of today's world financial system. By purchasing government debt, banks can allow the state—for a while—to finance its activities without taxation. On the surface, this appears to be a "free lunch." But it's actually quite pernicious and is the engine of currency debasement.

Central banks may seem like a permanent part of the cosmic landscape, but in fact they are a recent invention. The U.S. Federal Reserve, for instance, didn't exist before 1913.

Justin: What changed after 1913?

Doug: In the past, when a bank created too much currency out of nothing, people eventually would notice, and a "bank run" would materialize. But when a central bank authorizes all banks to do the same thing, that's less likely—unless it becomes known that an individual bank has made some really foolish loans.

Central banks were originally justified—especially the creation of the Federal Reserve in the US—as a device for economic stability. The occasional chastisement of imprudent bankers and their foolish customers was an excuse to get government into the banking business. As has happened in so many cases, an occasional and local problem was "solved" by making it systemic and housing it in a national institution. It's loosely analogous to the way the government handles the problem of forest fires: extinguishing them quickly provides an immediate and visible benefit. But the delayed and forgotten consequence of doing so is that it allows decades of deadwood to accumulate. Now when a fire starts, it can be a once-in-a-century conflagration.

Justin: This isn't just a problem in the US, either.

Doug: Right. Banking all over the world now operates on a "fractional reserve" system. In our earlier example, our sound banker kept a 100% reserve against demand deposits: he held one ounce of gold in his vault for every one-ounce banknote he issued. And he could only lend the proceeds of time deposits, not demand deposits. A "fractional reserve" system can't work in a free market; it has to be legislated. And it can't work where banknotes are redeemable in a commodity, such as gold; the banknotes have to be "legal tender" or strictly paper money that can be created by fiat.

The fractional reserve system is why banking is more profitable than normal businesses. In any industry, rich average returns attract competition, which reduces returns. A banker can lend out a dollar, which a businessman might use to buy a widget. When that seller of the widget re-deposits the dollar, a banker can lend it out at interest again. The good news for the banker is that his earnings are compounded several times over. The bad news is that, because of the pyramided leverage, a default can cascade. In each country, the central bank periodically changes the percentage reserve (theoretically, from 100% down to 0% of deposits) that banks must keep with it, according to how the bureaucrats in charge perceive the state of the economy.

Justin: How can a default cascade under the fractional reserve banking system?

Doug: A bank with, say, $1,000 of capital might take in $20,000 of deposits. With a 10% reserve, it will lend out $19,000—but that money is redeposited in the system. Then 90% of that $19,000 is also lent out, and so forth. Eventually, the commercial bank can create hundreds of thousands of loans. If only a small portion of them default, it will wipe out the original $20,000 of deposits—forget about the bank's capital.

That's the essence of the problem. But, in the meantime, before the inevitable happens, the bank is coining money. And all the borrowers are thrilled with having dollars.

Justin: Are there measures in place to prevent bank runs?

Doug: In the US and most other places, protection against runs on banks isn't provided by sound practices, but by laws. In 1934, to restore confidence in commercial banks, the US government instituted the Federal Deposit Insurance Corporation (FDIC) deposit insurance in the amount of $2,500 per depositor per bank, eventually raising coverage to today's $250,000. In Europe, €100,000 is the amount guaranteed by the state.

FDIC insurance covers about $9.3 trillion of deposits, but the institution has assets of only $25 billion. That's less than one cent on the dollar. I'll be surprised if the FDIC doesn't go bust and need to be recapitalized by the government. That money—many billions—will likely be created out of thin air by selling Treasury debt to the Fed.

The fractional reserve banking system, with all of its unfortunate attributes, is critical to the world's financial system as it is currently structured. You can plan your life around the fact the world's governments and central banks will do everything they can to maintain confidence in the financial system. To do so, they must prevent a deflation at all costs. And to do that, they will continue printing up more dollars, pounds, euros, yen, and what-have-you.

Justin: It sounds like the banking system is more fragile than it was a decade ago... not stronger.

Doug: Correct. So, Yellen isn't just delusional. As I said before, she has no grasp whatsoever of basic economics.

Her comments remind me of what Ben Bernanke said in May 2007.

We believe the effect of the troubles in the subprime sector on the broader housing market will likely be limited, and we do not expect significant spillovers from the subprime market to the rest of the economy or to the financial system.

A few months later, the entire financial system started to unravel. You would have actually lost a fortune if you listened to Bernanke back then.

Justin: I take it investors shouldn't listen to Yellen, either?

Doug: No. These people are all academics. They don't have any experience in the real world. They've never been in business. They were taught to believe in Keynesian notions. These people have no idea what they're talking about.

The Fed itself serves no useful purpose. It should be abolished.

But people look up to authority figures, and "experts." The average guy has other things on his mind.

Justin: So if Yellen's wrong, what should investors prepare for? How will the coming crisis be different from what we saw in 2007–2008?

Doug: Well, as you know, the Fed has dropped interest rates to near zero. I used to think it was metaphysically impossible for rates to drop below zero. But the European and Japanese central banks have done it.

The other thing they did was create megatons of money out of thin air. This hasn't just happened in the U.S., either. Central banks around the world have printed up trillions of currency units.

How many more can they print at this point? I guess we'll find out. Plus, it's not like these dollars have gone to the retail economy the way they did during the "great inflation" of the '70s. This time they went straight into the financial system. They've created bubbles everywhere.

That's why the next crisis is going to be far more serious than what we saw a decade ago.

Justin: Is there anything the Fed can do to stop this? What would you do if you were running the Fed?

Doug: I've been saying for years that I would abolish the Fed, end the fractional reserve system, and default on the national debt. But would I actually do any of those things? No. I wouldn't. I pity the poor fool who allows the rotten structure to collapse on his watch. Perish the thought of bringing it down in a controlled demolition.

They would literally crucify the person who did this... even if it was good for the economy in the long run. Which it would be.

So, these people are going to keep doing what they've been doing. They're hoping that, if they kick the can down the road, something magic will happen. Maybe friendly aliens will land on the roof of the White House and cure everything.

Justin: So, they can't stop what's coming?

Doug: The whole financial system is on the ragged edge of a collapse at this point.

All these paper currencies all around the world could lose their value together. They're all based on the dollar quite frankly. None of them are tied to any commodity.

They have no value in and of themselves, aside from being mediums of exchange. They're all just floating abstractions, based on nothing.

When we exit the eye of this financial hurricane, and go into the storm's trailing edge, it's going to be something for the history books written in the future.

Doug Casey on the Illinois Debt Crisis

―――――

ORIGINALLY PUBLISHED ON JUNE 30, 2017

Justin's note: Illinois is dead broke. Every month, it spends $600 million more than it collects in taxes. The state is now $15 billion in debt. There's no telling how much worse its financial situation will become, either. After all, Illinois hasn't had a budget in two years. If it can't put one together by tomorrow, Standard & Poor's will cut its credit rating to "junk." It would become the first state ever with this distinction. This would have serious implications for the 13 million people living in Illinois. It could trigger a nationwide debt crisis…

Justin: Doug, what do you make of Illinois' debt crisis?

Doug: It's absolutely wonderful.

Perhaps this brings out a little bit of the quasi-Leninist in me, because Lenin said "the worse it gets, the better it gets." I'd like to see all of the states go bankrupt for the same reasons I said the federal government should default on its debt[1].

Most of what all levels of government do is usurped from society. Assuming you even accept the principle of legal coercion—I don't—there's very little that a government should do.

Justin: What sort of things should the government not do?

Doug: Education, for one.

The numbers vary, but typically it costs about $12,000 per year to educate a grade school student. It's a completely absurd amount. Most of it is wasted on administration, bureaucracy, compliance, and overhead. But that's not the point.

The point is that the state shouldn't be in charge of kids' education, because inevitably it turns into indoctrination. Teachers work for their employer, the gov-

―――――

1. www.caseyresearch.com/doug-casey-on-hunger-bonds/

ernment. The interests of the government are not necessarily those of either the children or the parents. State education works on the premise that parents are in general too ignorant and irresponsible to care for their progeny. And maybe that's true—the proof being that they're willing to send kids off to be incarcerated and indoctrinated by government employees for eight hours a day.

The bankruptcy of Illinois might push things in the direction of privatization and localization of education. Local schools generally get State and Federal funds, and have to obey State and Federal rules. Education necessarily becomes rote, non-innovative, PC, and one-size-fits-all. Teachers, which are less and less necessary in the Internet world, are roboticized and disincentivized.

The roads are another big State function. And a huge source of featherbedding, incompetence, and corruption. All the roads should be privatized, quite frankly. Local roads should be the province of something like homeowners associations. Thoroughfares should be toll roads. And with today's computer technology, it would be very easy to do that.

Justin: Don't forget public pensions. In the case of Illinois, its public pension is underfunded to the tune of $126 billion.

Illinois isn't the only state with pension problems, either. Credit rating agency Moody's estimates that U.S. state pension plans are underfunded by nearly $1.8 trillion.

Doug: State employees are notorious, during their last year or two or three, depending on how their benefits are determined, for padding their salaries with lots of overtime. Their buddies give them promotions when possible, so they can check out with the largest possible pension.

This would be much less likely it was a private company. Why? Because everyone naturally views the state as a milk cow, but private companies are oriented strictly to make profits.

What should be done with the pensioners who are relying on pensions which can't be paid? Well, it's a question for a bankruptcy court to answer. But in most bankruptcies, the debtor's assets are sold off to pay for its obligations. In the case of Illinois—and other states that will soon find themselves in the same position—that means their assets should be auctioned off and privatized. And all of its responsibilities should be taken away as well. A genuine bankruptcy of the state government would prove a very good thing.

Very little that the state government does serves much useful purpose. The services they provide that are needed and wanted could be, and would be, provided much more efficiently by entrepreneurs. The DMV is typical of the way government works. We might first ask: Is a DMV actually needed in the first place?

But back to the pensions. If, after asset liquidations, the pensions have to be cut back or defaulted on? Tough. There's no reason people who are employed by the state should have special privileges.

This isn't a theoretical discussion. Most pensions are in serious jeopardy. Why? Because their assets are mostly in bonds and stocks. The stock market is in a bubble. The bond market is in a super bubble. A lot of the value of the assets could disappear. Most projections of asset gain have been set to high, in order to reduce current funding requirements. Furthermore, people are living longer today than most actuaries projected when the pensions were set up.

From a pensioner's point of view, things are not going to improve. It's going to get worse, not better. I don't see any way out of this.

Justin: I agree, Doug.

The pension system is not as safe as many people think. Thanks to the Federal Reserve, it's more dangerous than ever.

That's because eight years of easy money have made it nearly impossible for pension funds to make money in "safe" assets. So, they've loaded up on stocks, which are riskier than bonds. They've even piled into private equity investments. That used to be unheard of.

Doug: Yeah, absolutely. Pension payments aren't "guaranteed" by the cosmos, or the laws of physics. Especially when you're living in a financial bubble, like the one that's been created by the Fed and other central banks.

And here's a revelation: I like living in a financial bubble. It's pleasant. You have a higher standard of living than you might otherwise, because you're living out of other people's capital that they've saved in the past. And you're borrowing from the future. An artificially high standard of living may be stupid and artificial—but it still feels good.

It's a fool's paradise, sure. But most people don't realize that because they don't study either economics or history—they don't make the time, or have the interest, and have more pressing concerns. I hope the bubble goes on longer because I'm in a couple private deals. I'm anxious for them to go public because I'll make a lot of money if they IPO before the bubble breaks. If they don't, I'll probably get a goose egg.

So, I find myself cheering on the Fed—like everyone else with a lot of financial assets. At the same time, I'm well known as a bear. It's not that I'm cheering for the bubble to burst—that would be against my interests. I'm a bear because I know burst it will.

Anyway, back to the subject at hand. I have no sympathy at all for these state employees who will lose their pensions, and maybe their jobs. Most of whom haven't spent their lives "protecting and serving" the public—that's a PR fiction. But acting as parasites, although in many cases unknowingly.

So, I look forward to the bankruptcy of Illinois. It's absolutely inevitable. I hope that the US government doesn't step in and bail them out somehow, because there are other states that are going to be lining up behind them.

Justin: Could Illinois' debt problems spread to other states? If so, how do you see that shaking out?

Doug: It's got to spread because the markets are at an all-time high. When stocks and bonds go down, the pensions are going to have fewer assets to service their liabilities.

The silver lining of this—and I always like to look at the bright side of things—is that these states are going to have to fire 25% or 50% or 75% of their employees, and privatize most of the things that should have been in private hands to start with. You never really get a change in any system, unless there's a crisis.

Now the problem is: what will they do when a crisis comes? Will they do the intelligent thing—fire employees, default on a lot of these pensions, and sell assets? Or what's more likely I'm afraid, is that they'll double down, and try to raise taxes even further, get funding through the federal government, and make it even worse. But we're gonna have a crisis for sure. The only question is, how stupidly they'll react—really stupidly, or with a modicum of intelligence? Chances are it'll be the former.

It's like that fool who's the current mayor of Chicago said: "Never let a good crisis go to waste." The problem is that he, and people like him, see the crisis as an opportunity to devolve even more power to the state, not less. Exactly the opposite of what I'm proposing.

Justin: How would the federal government respond to this sort of crisis?

Doug: Well, the federal government is already running a $1 trillion deficit every year. I guess they can borrow even more money with interest rates as low as they are. But they can't sell paper to the Chinese anymore so they'll have to borrow it from the Federal Reserve, which means that they have to print more money.

What they'll likely do, therefore, is take a local problem in states like Illinois, and make it a national problem. It's not a solution at all, of course, but it's what they're going to do. It's called "kicking the can down the road," where it will be somebody else's problem.

Justin: If the government can't fix this, what is the solution? What can people in states like Illinois do to protect themselves?

Doug: I grew up in Illinois, I have a lot of friends that still live in Illinois, and it's a funny thing. It's that most people, even intelligent people, act like potted plants. They're born in one place, and they just don't like to move. Including my friends that grew up in Illinois. Most of them are still in Illinois—not because it's the best place, but because of inertia. So, what they should do is get the hell out of Illinois, and move to a state that's more fiscally responsible, that has no income taxes, like Nevada for instance. Or Washington, or Tennessee, or Florida. But most of them stay in Illinois.

Most people don't do what they "should" do. Most people just don't like to move. They're like the proverbial deer in the headlights.

Justin: And if it turns into a national crisis... what should people do then?

Doug: Well, I've been advocating that people internationalize themselves for years. Because your biggest risk today is not financial. Your financial risks are huge, with the markets and the economy the way they are. Your biggest risk is political. What is your government going to do to you, if it's to survive?

You've got to remember that the prime directive of any organism, whether it's an amoeba or a person or a corporation or a government, is to survive. So these governments are going to fight to survive. And the only way that they can survive is to tax more. And that's exactly what they're going to do.

Doug Casey on 100-Year Bonds

ORIGINALLY PUBLISHED ON JUNE 23, 2017

Justin's note: Argentina just issued a 100-year bond. That's not a typo. South America's second-biggest country issued a bond that matures 100 years from now. This is completely nuts. After all, a lot can happen over the course of a century. Not to mention, Argentina doesn't exactly have the best credit history. It's defaulted on its debt seven times since it was founded in 1816. Three of those defaults happened in the last 23 years. And yet, people lined up to buy these bonds...

Justin: Doug, what do you make of Argentina selling 100-year bonds?

Doug: These bonds are the 7.125's of 2117. They're selling US$2.75 billion of them, at around 90, priced to yield about 8%. The issue is apparently oversubscribed 3-1.

It's all quite amazing, from a number of points of view.

But first, I've got to say something about bonds in general, to set a context. As we speak right now, we're at the peak of probably the biggest bubble in history. Vastly bigger than the Tulipmania of the 17th century, the South Sea and Mississippi Bubbles of the 18th, and the '20s stock market bubble of the 20th combined. It's a super bubble. The current bond bubble will go down in history. As a catastrophe.

I used to think it was metaphysically impossible for interest rates to go below zero. But clearly with financial engineering absolutely anything is possible.

The very idea of buying almost any kind of bond in today's market impresses me as incredibly stupid. But buying a bond that goes out a hundred years is the type of thing that only happens at the top of a mania. And to top it off, it's with the government of Argentina...

The whole world—not just computers—is changing at the rate of Moore's Law.

Justin: I know you don't like buying government bonds because they fund wasteful governments. But what makes them such a lousy investment?

Doug: There are three things anyone who buys bonds should keep in mind, anytime. But especially now.

Number one is the interest rate risk. Interest rates are at an all-time low right now. So, there's only one way they can go: up. And there are all kinds of reasons why they will not only go up, but rise beyond levels that we saw in the early 1980s when the US government was paying almost 20 percent for money.

Number two is credit risk. Will you actually get the money back? This is the big problem with Argentina. Any Argentine government is inherently, congenitally untrustworthy. The reigning political meme here for the last 80 years has been Peronism. It's basically a fascist philosophy they adopted from Mussolini.

The State is involved in absolutely everything, all workers are unionized, most things are price controlled or subsidized, and so forth. That makes it very hard to predict anything about the economy, except that it's going to continue going downhill—certainly in relative terms. With real economic growth typically between -2% and 2%, how does anybody expect them to service 8% paper?

The third thing is the currency risk. Sure, you might get dollars back—but what will they be worth? If it was in Argentine pesos the bond would have been unsalable. Of course it's priced in US dollars. But the US government itself is bankrupt and running deficits of a trillion dollars per year. The dollar has lost like 80% of its value since 1971, and the trend will accelerate. The dollar is a floating abstraction. The prognosis is grim.

So, bonds in general are a triple threat to your capital in today's world. They're a trifecta of disastrous risk. That's the big picture.

I owned, and recommended, long maturity Treasuries, and many other bonds, in the '80s. But things today are quite different.

Justin: I'm with you on the interest rates and currency risks. But aren't things getting better in Argentina? If so, what makes these bonds so risky?

Doug: You know I love Argentina. I spend most of the year in Argentina. It's a fantastic lifestyle choice, but it's not a place where you can invest in anything other than property.

Owning real estate is fine; property rights for real estate are very good here. Because although it's the seventh largest country in the world, there are only 40 million people, and most of them live around Buenos Aires. The whole country is empty once you're out of BA. It's not a country like El Salvador, which is tiny and full of people. Here, you can still buy 100,000 acres of land for $1 million. It's not going to be very productive farm land, but it will be beautiful. Technology will make it quite valuable in the decades to come.

But back to the bonds. They'll eventually be worth zero. But might work out as speculation for the next couple of years.

Why? Because Mauricio Macri, the current president is doing, and has done already, a lot to make things better. He's probably the most decent person running any major government in the world today.

But making economic reforms in a country that's become corrupt because of so much state involvement means that there's a lot of pain—a lot of people are getting fired and a lot of uneconomic businesses going bust. So, what may happen is Macri fills the treasury until the next election in three years, at which point there's again something for the Kirchneristas or some other Peronists to steal. They'll promise the bounty that Macri has built up will be distributed to the people.

Justin: I see. So, you're optimistic about Argentina in the near term… but less optimistic over the next 100 years or so. Is that correct?

Doug: In the short run that $2.75 billion will feel good.

Some of it will be stolen with crony contracts and such, but since Macri isn't corrupt himself, most of it will be invested in infrastructure. As opposed to dissipated in freebee handouts to the people, and foreign bank accounts for the *nomenklatura*, which is what would have happened if the Kirchneristas had been reelected.

The money's going to improve the country. Debt always feels good—before you have to start paying the interest. But it's never going to be paid back for the reasons that I gave earlier. Maybe they'll be able to run up their foreign debt to $100 billion again, like they did the last time. Then it will truly be worth the aggravation of a default. In the meantime, it could be an OK short-term speculation as things look good for another couple of years, but it's a hot potato. Include me out.

Justin: Yeah, it seems that the only way to make money on these bonds is to sell them to someone else before they blow up in your face. In other words, you have to find a "greater fool."

Doug: To me, it's the bell ringing at the top of the market. I don't care if it's at eight percent interest. That people buy 100-year maturity bonds from not just Argentina but any government, you know it's the bell ringing at the top of the market. Just to show that the US can learn from Argentina, Mnuchin, the US Treasury Secretary, said he liked the idea. The US has been taking a lot of lessons from Argentina in recent years.

Justin: Argentina isn't the only country that's issued this crap, either. Mexico, the United Kingdom, and Ireland have issued 100-year bonds of their own. Giant multinational corporations like Walt Disney and Coca-Cola have also gotten in on the act.

What's fueling this, Doug?

Doug: There are two things.

One is low interest rates. Borrowing money today is like a gift.

The second thing is quantitative easing, the new name for currency inflation. Because there's no question that all world currencies are going to turn into toilet paper over the next 20 years.

In Buenos Aires, I have a fat envelope, full of currencies from various countries that I've visited in just the last decade. You always wind up with some banknotes that you didn't spend before you left… and already half of them are worth little or nothing from the level that I acquired them. Currencies from Cambodia, Vietnam, Bolivia, Seychelles, Mongolia—all these crazy places. The paper is essentially worthless. In fact even if I go back to these countries they probably won't even accept the banknotes, because they'll have changed them, even if the monetary unit still exists.

This happened in Europe to all the people that owned German marks, French francs and Italian lira a couple of years after the Euro came on. All those pieces of paper that you might have had stuffed away are worthless now, totally irredeemable. You can frame them as decorations for your wall—like most of the bonds governments have issued over the years.

All these governments are creating trillions and trillions of new currency units as we speak. Where's all that money going? Into the bond markets—like that of Argentina. It's crazy.

It's the bell ring at the top of the market when people will lend that government money for 100 years…

Justin: Exactly. You can add 100-year bonds to the long list of reasons for why you should own gold. Anyway, that's all I have for today. Thank you for sharing your insights, Doug.

Doug: Sure thing, Justin.

Doug Casey on "Hunger Bonds"

———

ORIGINALLY PUBLISHED ON JUNE 20, 2017

Justin's note: Goldman Sachs is in hot water. The investment bank recently bought around $2.8 billion worth of Venezuelan bonds. The bonds were issued by PDV-SA, Venezuela's national oil company, in 2014. And get this… Goldman paid just $865 million (or 31 cents on the dollar) for them. Goldman got such a sweet deal because Venezuela is in complete disarray right now…

Justin: Doug, what do you make of this? Did Goldman throw Venezuela a lifeline or was this just a savvy speculation on their end?

Doug: Well, several things should be considered here.

First, these bonds were bought in the aftermarket. So, no new money went to the Venezuelan government.

We did some research and they were 6% bonds. So, it seems to me like an excellent speculation on the part of Goldman because they're going to capture—if the bonds were trading at $0.31 on the dollar—a current return of almost 20%.

Plus, the increase in value in between now and 2022. Which should be a total return of 40% per year. At least if they keep interest payments current.

Let's look at this from a moral point of view. I'd say that people who buy new bonds from any government, including the US government, have a moral problem. They're directing capital from possibly productive areas of society to one which is almost always unproductive. So they're making the world poorer.

But speculation rarely includes moral philosophizing. And, since the bonds are trading in the aftermarket, ethics aren't an issue. The money doesn't go to the Venezuelan government, they're not selling the bonds. I think it's an excellent speculation on Goldman's part, however. If the Venezuelans default, Goldman will just file a suit to attach the issuer's assets anywhere in the world. Pretty much what happened with the Argentine government a while ago.

Now, as to the immorality of governments selling bonds, that's a different question. I know this sounds outrageous, but I've said for years that the US government should default on its bonds.

Justin: Why do you think that the US government should default on its debt?

Doug: Why? Number one, because I don't want to see the next generation, or several generations of Americans, turned into serfs to pay off those bonds, most of the capital for which has been wasted and dissipated by previous generations. So, that's one reason.

The second reason is that US government debt is going to be defaulted on eventually anyway, directly or indirectly. It's as if you have a hundred-story skyscraper that's about to collapse. It's better to have a controlled demolition to bring it down than just let it fall at random. It'll do a lot less damage. As a bonus, it would provide a good reason to auction off most of the governments assets to meet some of its liabilities.

A third reason, which perhaps relates more directly to the Venezuelan purchase, is to punish the buyers of government bonds, discouraging their future purchase.

Goldman expects that those bonds will be paid off in the future at par or close to it because if they're not, the Venezuelan government won't be able to borrow in the future. Or at least its national oil company won't. Of course the government essentially stole it from the previous shareholders. And every government with a state oil company uses it like a piggy bank—they're not run like sustainable businesses.

How will that be a problem? Governments shouldn't be able to borrow because they don't do anything productive with the money. Individual Venezuelan companies would still be able to borrow. People conflate all these things together. The government of a country is not the same thing as the people and the companies within the country's boundaries.

But while there's a real risk the Venezuelans will default, simply because they can't pay, there's about zero risk the US Government will ever do so. They can kick the can down the road for quite a while to come. The US dollar is the world's de facto currency, but the Venezuelan bolivar is worthless outside of Venezuela. And only accepted reluctantly within it.

Justin: Well said, Doug. Governments can only steal, destroy, and squander capital. So, the financial media shouldn't attack Goldman for buying Venezuelan oil bonds. They should attack anyone who finances wasteful and destructive governments, including US Treasury holders.

Now, aside from government bonds, are there any speculations that you consider immoral? Is there even such a thing?

Doug: That's a very good question, and I believe I have a very good answer.

I just finished writing, with John Hunt, the second novel in my High Ground series called *Drug Lord*, where we defend the morality of dealing drugs, and the right of individuals to take any drugs they wish. We explain the legal and illegal drug trades in some detail. There are many things that are perfectly moral—they may be stupid, but they're perfectly moral—that run counter to most people's views on these things.

But as far as investing in different countries, let me go back to what I said earlier. I'm happy to see people who buy government bonds punished, because they're supporting a destructive entity. It's a mistake to conflate support of one's country with support of the government.

But this is a personal decision that everybody has to make. A lot of people won't invest in tobacco producers or arms producers or god-knows-what. There are lots of different things that individuals consider immoral. It's a personal decision. Speaking as a speculator, however, that doesn't enter my mind. The only thing that enters my mind is what the risk/reward is, as opposed to the morality. It's a personal decision that everybody, including myself, has to make. But it's not a matter of public policy.

Justin: Before I let you go, Doug, I have to ask something…

Have you thought about speculating in Venezuela, personally? It looks like a huge crisis investing opportunity in the making.

Doug: Well, I've been to Venezuela at least four or five times over the years. It's potentially a great country, and I like it. I've gotten out of Caracas into the hinterlands several times too. It should not only be one of the world's richest countries, but one of the most pleasant to live in. It would be great to have a cattle ranch there. But property rights don't exist under the current government. If it's big, they'll likely steal the ranch. If it's small, they'll just steal the cattle. I wonder if you can even get a steak in a Caracas restaurant now.

The problem with a country like Venezuela is that they have one big resource: oil. And it's owned by the government. It becomes a piggy bank that everybody tries to raid and loot. Politics controls everything. The poverty-stricken mobs vote for the criminal that promises them the most freebies. It's like every other country in the world. But worse.

The country has been so corrupted over the years that nothing that you'd own there is really safe. It's a really good question: Would I want to buy in Venezuela as a crisis investment. Well, you can't "invest" in a place this chaotic, with such bad trends. But it might be an excellent speculation soon. Maduro won't last. The way to play it? Stocks, because they're liquid. We'll need to get boots on the ground soon.

Justin: That we will. Thanks for your insight, Doug.

Doug: My pleasure, Justin.

Doug Casey on Nuclear War With North Korea

—

ORIGINALLY PUBLISHED ON JULY 14, 2017

Justin's note: North Korea is "not far away" from launching an intercontinental ballistic missile (ICBM). That's the word coming out of Pyongyang, North Korea's capital. Bloomberg, The Wall Street Journal, and Reuters have all reported on it. It's a scary prospect, for sure. After all, North Korea's leader, Kim Jong-un, seems hell-bent on destroying the United States. At this point, one can't help but wonder if we could actually have a full-blown nuclear war on our hands…

Justin: Doug, could North Korea really launch an ICBM soon?

Doug: There's no question that even a dismally poor country like North Korea could do it.

Remember that ballistic missiles were first used in the 1940s by the Germans. A lot of things have happened in the last 70 years. The technology is widely disseminated, and the components are vastly improved. It's no longer "rocket science," as it were, to develop a missile.

But I don't know why people are paying so much attention to the development of a North Korean missile, because they're only important if you can put a nuclear weapon on them. Which they'll also be able to do. But who cares? At this point, ICBMs as a delivery system are old technology. You'd be stupid to use them.

If the North Koreans launched a nuclear missile attack, its source would be easily detected. It would be like signing their own death warrant. Nuclear weapons are a good counter-punch threat, to fend off an invasion—if Saddam had them the US wouldn't have dared to invade Iraq. But they make no sense as an aggressive weapon.

Justin: That's good to hear. But couldn't they launch a nuclear attack on the US using other means?

Doug: If they want to destroy a foreign city, be it Tokyo, Seoul or Los Angeles, the way to do it is to deliver the device by commercial ship, in a container. It could be set off in a number of ways, by GPS, by timer, or radio signal, among other obvious means. It could be delivered by a commercial airplane, which would get landing clearance, like any other plane.

And frankly, if they can miniaturize the things enough, have them delivered by FedEx; they'll arrive exactly where they're supposed to, cheaply, and on time. Which is more than an ICBM can promise.

As usual, the press is looking in all the wrong directions. And North Korea, developing ICBMs, is wasting its meager resources. If they really want to destroy cities—which is itself stupid and counterproductive, even as a counterpunch—they're looking at the previous technology. The way generals always do. It's like cavalry before World War I and battleships before World War II. ICBMs are in an exactly analogous position now. They're dinosaurs.

Justin: What are the chances that a nuke is actually set off?

Doug: Well, the US is said to have three carrier battle groups offshore North Korea. That's extremely provocative, as provocative as it would be if the Koreans had warships off the coast of California.

I think it's incredibly stupid for the US to do that; it serves no useful purpose. The NK government can use it as propaganda, to show their subjects how aggressive the Americans are. It's not a hard sale to make. The average American is unaware that during the Korean War, the US may have killed 20% of the NK population. The US totally flattened every city in the country with bombers. It doesn't win friends in a primitive country when an alien race comes in and basically destroys everything you have. The memory doesn't disappear overnight.

Provocations might push the North Koreans into doing something that they otherwise wouldn't.

That's one reason that a friend of mine who's one of the richest, and certainly one of the most well connected, men in the world, thinks this is going to end badly. He's quite thoughtful, and we've been friends for many, many years.

We were talking the other day; he spends a lot of time in the Orient, including Korea. He thinks there's an 80 percent chance that there will be some type of nuclear exchange. That's a high number. And it seems to me like a reasonable prediction based upon the psychologies of Kim Jong-un and Donald Trump.

Extremely dangerous situation, and who can say where it would end if there was a nuclear exchange. Or if the US decided to take out some nuclear facilities in North Korea using nuclear weapons.

Justin: Yeah, I can only imagine how quickly this situation would spiral out of control.

Doug: How can anyone predict what comes next when one nuclear bomb goes off in Korea? Perhaps they already have plans to deliver on their own nuclear devices in South Korea or Japan or for that matter in the US, likely using methods that we talked about earlier.

When that happens, the US would counterattack, and turn the place into a smoking ruin. Maybe the Chinese get involved because North Korea is right on their border.

These things can spin out of control in much the way trivial events before World War I spun out of control. And it seems to me that the world is a powder keg now, very much as it was before an accident set off World War I. The smart thing for the US is to withdraw their "tripwire" divisions from Korea, Japan, and elsewhere. All they'll do is turn a regional conflict into WW3. And the 7th fleet sailing around the South and East China Seas? It's analogous to the Chinese Navy holding maneuvers in the Gulf of Mexico.

It's an idiotic conceit to say it's "keeping the peace." In fact it's asking for trouble.

Justin: How would a nuclear exchange impact global financial markets? I can't see it being the type of thing that investors brush off.

Doug: I can't see how it could have any good ramifications at all, because if there's a war, it's going to destroy a huge amount of wealth, number one. Wars are all about killing people and destroying property. The longer it lasts, the worse it will be. The US has alliances with almost every government on the globe—with the obvious exceptions. The US Government is already bankrupt; they'll borrow, inflate, and tax more if they expand their current wars. And become much bigger and more powerful.

It's got to be a bad thing for the stock market. Even if a bunch of mushroom clouds don't appear over US cities.

Furthermore, you don't know who's going to win the war, or what even constitutes winning for that matter. You remember what Einstein said when asked what weapons WW3 would be fought with? He said he didn't know, but thought WW4 would be fought with sticks and stones.

I've always been a gold bug for lots of both economic and philosophical reasons—since gold was $35.00 an ounce quite frankly. And right now, in the midst of a stock market bubble, a real estate bubble, and a bond market super-bubble, the most important thing is preservation of capital.

So that's why you buy gold. I think that there's real upside in gold—although, in real terms, nothing like we've seen in the past. The main reason you buy it is to preserve capital. That keeps it simple.

You may not be able to preserve capital by owning cash, which is just fiat dollars, and holding it in banks, almost all of whom are bankrupt, all around the world. You can speculate in the stock market today, but at current levels, and with the world the way it is, it's a speculation, not an investment.

That's the problem with a highly politicized world. I'll like the stock market more when it's again yielding at least 5% or 6%. In the past, major markets have yielded in the 10-15% range at bottoms.

Justin: Absolutely. Of course, North Korea is just one of many reasons why investors should own physical gold if they don't already.

Anyway, thank you for taking the time to speak me with today.

Doug: My pleasure, Justin.

Doug Casey on Cultural Appropriation

———

ORIGINALLY PUBLISHED ON JUNE 12, 2017

Justin's note: White people shouldn't make burritos. At least, that's what some people in Portland think... It all started after two white women from Portland took a road trip to Mexico. There, they met the "tortilla ladies" of Puerto Nuevo. They asked about their process... learned their basic ingredients... and watched them roll tortillas from scratch. When the two women returned to Portland, they opened their own restaurant, Kooks Burritos, using what they'd learned. They also shared the story of their Mexican road trip with a local publication. A week after that story broke, their restaurant shut down due to accusations of "cultural appropriation[1]." In other words, it's apparently racist to replicate another culture's cuisine...

Justin: Doug, what did you make of this story? Does the punishment fit the "crime"?

Doug: This actually beggars the imagination that a couple of girls take a trip to Mexico, improve their cooking skills—and are punished for it. And apparently not by Mexicans living in Portland, but apparently by other white people, since Portland is a very white city. Although it's impossible to determine from press reports the racial makeup of the protestors. In today's ultra-PC world, reporters wouldn't mention that unless it seemed to prove that whites were oppressing non-whites.

It's safe to conjecture, however, that there's a cadre of activists who make their living by being professional brown or black people, who've rounded up some self-hating whites to act as their running dogs. The tactic has worked well for "community organizers" like Al Sharpton and Barack Obama.

People that perceive themselves as being underprivileged, or minorities, or Peo-

---

1. http://fxn.ws/2rjlu0L

ple of Color, or whatever they want to call themselves, have captured the semantic and philosophical high ground. At this point, however, these people (am I being non-PC in using that phrase? Maybe… it's so hard to stay current) aren't driven by any rationality for things done to them, or their ancestors. They're just being driven by hatred, envy, and avarice. A civilization is in trouble when vices have captured the philosophical high ground.

It's as if it's become a bad thing to be a white person. Which is rather amazing, because essentially all of the things that make life easy and pleasant—science, literature, music, inventions, industry, technology—have been created by white Europeans. Today, however, it's considered shameful to be of European extraction. White people supposedly aren't allowed to take advantage of the very few things that Third Worlders actually have produced.

So it seems to me that, at the very time community organizers and the chattering classes are accusing whites of racism, we're actually building towards some kind of a serious race war. One that they're actively trying to foment, at least as much as the Ku Klux Klan ever did. Which is really a pity, because personally, I choose my friends based upon their character and what they do, not based on some accident of birth.

At the same time, it's got to be said that ever since humans became biologically modern about 100,000 years ago—although anthropologists are starting to think it may be as long as 300,000–500,000 years ago—anybody from an outside group that looked different or dressed differently was viewed with suspicion. Because they might be pursuing the same deer that you are. And maybe the only thing you had in common was the deer that you both wanted to kill and take home for dinner. That was the start of racism, or "my groupism." If you look different, you're not part of my group. If you're not part of my group, you're probably an enemy. Which was probably, factually, the case in the days of scarce resources.

Racism, therefore, isn't entirely irrational. And it's probably a genetic characteristic at this point. "Discrimination" is necessary and laudable; it's entirely a question of how rational it is.

Justin: But Doug, humans no longer have to fight each other for meals to survive. And yet, racism seems to be getting worse.

Doug: Yes, it's perverse that at the very time when resources are becoming vastly more abundant that racism seems to be becoming more of an issue, not less of an issue. This is very disturbing. Racism itself is a perfectly natural thing, and has survival value. But race hatred, which is what these people are fomenting, makes no sense. Neither does making laws against it make any sense.

I prefer that people be at liberty to openly express their beliefs, and the state of their psyches. Not have to cover these things up. I like to know whom I'm dealing with…

Perhaps the reason we're seeing a resurgence of race hatred is that these people have spent most of their lives in government schools, and have been inculcated with Cultural Marxism. Because the schools seem to be getting worse, I don't see that the situation is going to get better.

Justin: I agree, Doug. This kind of thinking is incredibly destructive. Can you imagine if people thought like this in the 1950s or '60s? We wouldn't have rock and roll, which came from the blues. The Rolling Stones might have been crucified.

Doug: Very good point. A free man can say what he thinks, and an honest man thinks what he says. Today's PC culture is making it hard not to act like a hypocritical slave. It's disgusting. And another sign of the ongoing collapse of Western Civilization.

Justin: At the end of the day, cultures borrow from each other. This is how society evolves. Yet, a growing number of people can't seem to grasp this. It's comical as much as it is disturbing.

Doug: This is the kind of thinking that wound up making people serfs, where if you were born in one place and one occupation, you were obligated to stay there. You weren't allowed to borrow from somebody else or learn a different trade, you were only supposed to do what tradition dictated. So I guess in PC World only blacks are supposed to make chitlins, and eat collard greens and watermelon, and only Mexicans are supposed to make burritos and tacos. I suppose the French aren't supposed to cook German food, either. Etc., etc.

It reminds me of that stupid meme Bush created, where "French fries" were renamed "Freedom fries" during the Gulf War. The whole thing is crazy. These people are criminally insane. As well as stupid.

It's like the minorities need protection because they're stupid and incompetent. And the white people will steal their cuisine from them, like they, idiotically, think they've stolen everything else. But if you look at it that way, these people have in fact stolen all the inventions of white people. Which is to say, just about everything you have in the world that's worth having today. It's a sign of psychological aberration. There's absolutely no intellectual, moral, or any other argument that can be made for this stupidity. But it's growing, not diminishing.

Trends in motion tend to stay in motion, until a crisis happens. Then a new trend evolves. But who's to say the new trend is going to be better than this one? It might be worse.

Justin: Yes, unfortunately, this isn't just a problem in Portland. It's a nationwide epidemic.

Doug: It's a good argument for why the US should break up into little sub-countries. And the breakup should be done on cultural grounds. Because the people of Portland have very little in common with the ranchers in eastern Oregon. Just like the people in San Francisco and Los Angeles have very little in common with the people in the California desert and farm country. And the people who live in pot country in Mendocino County have very little in common with the people that live in San Diego. It's ridiculous that California be one state. It should be several.

The same is true of most states in the US, and the US as a whole, quite frankly. They're historic artifacts. They have very little reason for existence. And it's also true of most countries in the world, and I'm very gratified to see Catalonia making real efforts to break off from Spain. Part of the same problem. This is a cultural thing. There are no political solutions to cultural problems.

Justin: So, if the government can't fix this, what can? Is there even a cure?

Doug: That's a good question. It'll only get worse if the government makes more laws to "solve" this problem. And I don't know they'll ever even see the real problem. As they pass more laws, they're inevitably going to either aggravate the situation or clamp down on the pressure cooker so the explosion will be even bigger.

I'm glad to be here in South America most of the time. We don't have these problems in Argentina. Well, we do, but they're not as serious. Perhaps because this is a fairly culturally homogeneous country.

A final parenthetical note. Years ago I spent a week in Acapulco, staying at a house owned by a rich friend of mine in Hong Kong. In his visitor's book, he noted that there weren't any good Mexican restaurants in the city. Shockingly, he was right. Maybe that was because all the best chefs had emigrated to the US, or Mexico was then too poor to afford good ingredients for its own cuisine, or whatever, I don't know. But, in my experience, Americans have improved Mexican food. That's what "fusion" cuisine is all about, and I love it.

"Authentic" food from backward places—whatever its merits—is often unsanitary, coarse, unreliably prepared, and made from often questionable local materials. I've eaten plenty around the world, and native cuisines are almost always greatly improved when they're done over in America.

Let me hasten to add that I expect hate mail from Social Justice Warriors who occasionally troll this site, and believe anything from the primitive world is corrupted when it lands in the US. But I look forward to reading hate mail. It's more amusing than watching Comedy Central.

Justin: It sounds like you made the right decision by relocating to Argentina. If this keeps up, I might have to follow in your footsteps.

Anyway, that's all I got for you today. Thank you, Doug.

Doug: My pleasure, Justin.

Doug Casey on Crisis Investing in Brazil

ORIGINALLY PUBLISHED ON JUNE 9, 2017

Justin's note: Brazil is in crisis once again. This time, Brazil's president, Michel Temer, has been accused of corruption, bribery, and obstruction of justice. When news of this scandal broke, it triggered a huge selloff in Brazilian stocks. Most investors now want nothing to do with Brazilian stocks. But crises can actually lead to huge moneymaking opportunities…

Justin: Doug, what do you make of Brazil's latest crisis? Do you see a crisis investing opportunity shaping up there?

Doug: I'm not sure I'm interested in putting money there right now. But I am interested in Brazil.

As a matter of fact, as I speak to you right now, I'm out in the countryside of Uruguay, next door to Brazil. All these Latin American countries, quite frankly, are very problematical. They're all very state-oriented. All of them have extremely high levels of taxes and regulations. I'm just surprised that Latin America has done as well as it has, quite frankly. But it could have done much, much better.

Looking at Brazil in particular, I wrote <u>a long article on Brazil</u>[1] in *The Casey Report* in January of 2013, when three books had come out saying that Brazil finally turned the corner. That it's going to realize its potential. Everybody was ultra-optimistic, and the stock market was bubbly. A spate of books or magazine covers—bullish or bearish—are always a tipoff.

There's this old saying: "Brazil is the country of the future. And always will be." It's worse than Argentina in terms of taxes and regulations and corruption. Frankly, I don't know how anyone can do a legitimate business there. In terms of inflation,

---

1. www.internationalman.com/articles/evaluating-brazil

Brazil is even worse than Argentina. As late as the 1920's, however, they both had currencies redeemable in gold coins. Since then they've both replaced their currencies several times, with compounded inflation numbers in the many trillions.

Justin: So I take it you're not buying Brazil on the dips?

Doug: I see Brazil mainly as a speculative opportunity. The time will come when Brazilian stocks have high dividend yields and low P/E [price-to-earnings] ratios. I'll be happy to buy Brazilian stocks, someday. There are a couple dozen that trade in the US. There used to be Brazil Fund, on the NYSE. It was an especially good vehicle since, as a closed end fund, it could sell at either a big premium or a big discount to its assets. Predictably, it was a big premium when people were bullish, and a big discount when they were bearish. It's a real pity closed end funds have been mostly replaced by ETFs that always trade right at their asset values. The one for Brazil is the iShares MSCI Capped ETF (EWZ).

Incidentally, I'm a fan of Argentina now, because of [Mauricio] Macri being in office. Whether he can break the logjam and free up Argentina or not is very questionable—although he's done an immense amount so far, and seems a decent human being. On the other hand, maybe all he's really going to do is just refill the treasury during his term in office so there's something to steal for the next Kirchner government—or the next Kirchner lookalikes that come into office. That's the problem with all Third World countries.

You can't really "invest" in any of these countries. You can't invest in Brazil. You can only speculate in these countries. So I'm very interested, but the timing is not right yet.

Incidentally, the first time I thought about Brazil was when I was a kid, collecting stamps. I noticed some had multiple zeroes for the currency, for postage. Then, in college, I considered driving a car down there, to sell for a multiple of its US price because of the huge duties all the South American countries had—still have, actually—and escaping on a banana boat, or the like. And I remember reading, at the same time, about Daniel K. Ludwig, an American who was then one of the world's richest men, who bought 1.6 million acres of Amazon jungle for $3 million in 1967. It was still possible to do that sort of thing then. Of course that's still only like $20–25 million today. He wanted to make it into a pulp plantation. It was a disaster.

Justin: Aside from Brazil and Argentina, what other countries are on your radar? Any other crisis investing opportunities we should know about?

Doug: Well, I spent a week in Haiti in April when I was talking to mostly high government officials. Now, Haiti is the basket case of the Western Hemisphere—and one of the worst basket cases in the world. The investment possibilities? Absolutely zero, unless they radically change the basic structure of their whole economy, which means radically changing the way the government relates to their society.

But these backward countries are quite entertaining. I was in Zimbabwe last year doing the same thing, looking at business as well as talking to the government. Once again, it's the exact same problem. The income of the average Haitian, or Zimbabwean, or Brazilian was about the same as that of the average Singaporean or Hong Kong person back in the 60's. Since then the average in the first three has gone nowhere, but in Singapore and HK everybody is getting rich. It's all a matter of what the government does—and doesn't—do.

Justin: Do you plan to visit any other backward countries like Haiti and Zimbabwe in the near future?

Doug: Chances are good that in the next few months, I'll be going to Angola, Guinea (Conakry), the Democratic Republic of the Congo, and/or Mozambique. All of them are hopeless basket cases. All crisis-type places, totally impossible for investment. In other words, the only way you can put money in those places is on a hit-and-run basis. It's impossible and idiotic to try to "invest" in those countries.

The only kind of entrepreneurship that exists in those countries is political entrepreneurship, or perhaps finding some way that you can import or export something. But trying to produce something within the country? Almost a non-starter in most of these countries. It's one of the reasons that make me pessimistic on the world in general, because most of the actionable innovation and production and capital accumulation in the world takes place in North America, Japan, and parts of Europe. The populations of those places—and I should add China and South Korea—are aging rapidly.

But, more important, the whole world is slowing down as these countries start to more and more resemble the old Soviet Union. More political correctness, with more rules, more regulations, more bureaucracy, higher taxes, unstable currencies, and fewer property rights.

As always, I'm of two minds. The good news is there are more scientists and engineers alive today than have lived in all the world's history put together. And they're continuing to do fantastic things, which are improving life. But at the same time, you've got a countertrend, a slow collapse of Western Civilization that started in about 1914.

Which is going to succeed, and over what time frame? I don't know, but how to answer the question: What's the best crisis investment in the world today? I'm not sure I'd look for one until there's a big crisis in the US. My view is that we're still in the eye of the hurricane that we've been in since the leading edge of the storm started in 2007. And as we go into the trailing edge, we're going to have big crises all over the place. We're going to have more crises than we'll know what to do with.

The thing to do right now is to keep your powder dry. Being in the stock and bond markets is like picking up seashells on the beach when the tide goes out just before a tsunami. This isn't the time to go looking for a crisis, because we don't have one just at the moment.

Justin: Great insights as always, Doug. Thank you for taking the time to speak with me.

Doug: Anytime, Justin.

Doug Casey on Universal Basic Income

ORIGINALLY PUBLISHED ON JUNE 3, 2017

Justin's note: It's time for a universal basic income (UBI). A UBI is a form of social security in which citizens receive a regular, unconditional sum of money from the government. At least, that's what Mark Zuckerberg thinks. Zuckerberg is the founder and CEO of social media giant Facebook. He recently spoke in favor of a universal basic income while delivering the commencement speech at Harvard's graduation ceremony. He says this generation owes a UBI to society. But a UBI would have serious ramifications for society...

Justin: Doug, what do you make of Zuckerberg's suggestion? Is it time for a UBI?

Doug: It's incredibly stupid from absolutely every point of view. He makes statements like "every generation expands its definition of equality," as if it was a fact. Which it's not. And as if it's a good thing, which it's not. He talks of "a new social contract"—which is code for somebody on high telling you what to do.

If "society"—whoever that's supposed to be—were to push for any values, equality shouldn't be among them. Equality only exists before the law. People are unique, and therefore naturally unequal. We're not like ants or blades of grass. Equality is not only impossible, it's not even desirable. A proper goal to strive for is freedom, which is possible and desirable.

These people don't seem to compute that no one has a right to anything just because they exist.

Now, they'll say, "Well, it's not being taken from somebody else because a robot is producing it." But somebody created the robot. Somebody invested in that robot. Somebody owns the robot. And when production is diverted from further wealth creation and given over to consumption, that's likely a misallocation of capital. The same basic argument could have been made with every labor saving device that's ever been invented—the plow, the loom, the steam engine. A million things. If you immediately consume—as opposed to save—any excess of production, it's impossible to grow in wealth. That's point number one.

But that's mainly an economic argument, and few people understand economics—so it won't convince anyone. People don't *think* when it comes to these things. They feel. Let me address even more important flaws in the Zuck's reasoning.

Recall that wonderful IBM meme: "Machines should work, people should think." It's absolutely true. But a problem arises when people take the unearned. And there are a lot of people that, if they don't have to produce, won't produce. They become what Lenin used to call "useless mouths."

Zuckerberg says he wants to see that "everyone has a cushion to try new ideas." He's making a political speech, not describing reality, and apparently has zero understanding of human nature. 99% of people will spend their "cushion" and their free time following celebrities or chasing the opposite sex, not researching "new ideas."

Justin: But aren't robots taking people's jobs? What are most people supposed to do if this trend continues?

Doug: People say, "When robots are producing everything, we're not going to need factory workers. We may not need most jobs because of artificial intelligence, which will do most things that aren't creative. Most things will be done by robots." And I'd say that's wonderful. However it doesn't mean that people will all become supernumeraries. We're all basically lazy—it's genetic. Both our bodies and our psyches are programmed to conserve energy. It's a key to survival. But should people be encouraged, via a UBI, to become Eloi, being fed by robot Morlocks? Incidentally, I hope the term "UBI" doesn't become a meme—the thought is often father to the reality.

If a machine can replace you: Great! It means you were doing dog work, robot work. That's why 90% of the population no longer have to work in the fields every day. I have no doubt that, in the future, the average man will have more options than Zuckerberg does now, because the world will become vastly wealthier—just as the average man today lives vastly better than any medieval king. And it's going to happen soon. But it's not going to happen because someone on top is distributing alms to the peasants.

The key question is this: Absolutely every human being—you and me and everybody else—has an infinite number of desires. If you have one Ferrari, maybe you want 10 because they're fun to collect. If you have a summer house, maybe you want a winter house. Desires are unlimited. Everybody wants everything. Everybody wants more. Unless you're an ascetic monk—but that's another topic. So there's zero need for unemployment. You could work 24/7 fulfilling the wants of other humans. They're infinite.

What I'm trying to say is there's an infinite demand for goods and services, and it can never be fulfilled—I don't care how many robots you have. And I'd like to see a billion of them…

Furthermore, giving people a subsistence income—a UBI—has been tried extensively in Europe and the US. Saudi Arabia basically has a UBI, and it's a social and political time bomb, in part because of it. Since Johnson's Great Society programs of the '60s, you can get free food, free schooling, free housing, free medical care—through scores of welfare programs. All those things have done is cement their "beneficiaries"—mainly poor blacks—to the bottom of society. Most of the poor people in the ghettoes and trailer parks already have UBIs—it's called welfare. It hasn't improved things; it's destroyed society wherever it was implemented. So far UBI hasn't created a class of artists and philosophers, it's created a class of derelicts and criminals.

It's a matter of psychology even more than economics. Unearned stuff doesn't just destroy most poor people, it also destroys most rich people. Has the UBI, in the form of large inheritances, made the kids of the rich into better or happier people? Sometimes—if their parents have good values. But usually not. They're "enabled" to become spoiled brats, of no use to either themselves or other people.

If a true UBI was put into effect, productive people are going to find it degrading, and unproductive people are going to take advantage of it. More important, it's immoral, because you're taking production from some people and giving it to others that have done nothing in return to deserve it. That creates resentment. Simply being alive doesn't give you the right to demand things from other people.

It's a scary thought that somebody like Zuckerberg—who, frankly, is just a guy with some business skills who got lucky—is positioning himself to run for president. If people think that Trump is bad, wait until somebody like Zuckerberg gets into office.

Justin: Zuckerberg isn't the only billionaire championing for a universal basic income, either.

Tesla founder and CEO Elon Musk also thinks we should have it. According to Musk, UBI is needed now because we're entering "post-scarcity economy." Do you think a post-scarcity economy is even possible?

Doug: I have no doubt that—barring World War 3, or serious socialism—it's definitely going to be possible to provide a subsistence for everybody. At somebody's expense. I suspect Musk is right when he says that some day we'll have replicators, like those on *Star Trek*. Nanotech may make that possible, and a real Cornucopia might come into existence. But it's a question of motivation as to whether people produce, or vegetate. If people don't have to produce, perhaps they're going to become even more zombielike and more robotic than they are today. Will the average person turn his mind to great art and philosophy and literature? That's doubtful, based on what's happened so far with welfare.

The most important thing to look at, however, is not the technical ramifications of UBI—whether it's technically possible. A bigger question is who allocates these things. Because, obviously, it's going to direct more power to the government. They'll determine how the fruits of all this get distributed.

It's not, however, going to make for a more equal society. It's going to make a more unequal society. But the inequality won't be based upon productive people getting things by working and saving. It will be based on how much political pull they have. These people love to politicize things.

So, to wrap this up, a guaranteed income, a UBI, not only won't solve the so-called equality problem, it's actually going to create more social antagonism. Because more resources will be diverted to the State, so the State can give everyone what they think is a "just" UBI. The best case is that it will only slow down progress—because unearned income will be directed towards unproductive people, probably encouraging them to be even more unproductive. The worst case is that it will accelerate the collapse of civilization as both rich and poor are turned into HG Wells' Eloi, given goodies by technocratic Morlocks like Musk and Zuckerberg.

The UBI, if it's implemented somehow, has the potential to reverse the Ascent of Man. It's a stupid and retrograde idea from every point of view. But a surprising number of really stupid ideas have been produced by smart people. They see themselves as visionary problem solvers, but they're really just busybodies.

Justin: Brilliant insights as always, Doug. Thank you for your time.

Doug: My pleasure, Justin.

Doug Casey on Robots and the Federal Debt

ORIGINALLY PUBLISHED ON JUNE 2, 2017

Justin's note: Could robots wipe out the federal debt? Robert Atkinson thinks so. Atkinson is the president of the Information Technology and Innovation Foundation, a nonprofit based in Washington D.C. According to his research, robots could soon quintuple the U.S. economic growth rate. He says this would generate enough tax revenue to pay off the federal debt. It's a radical idea, for sure. After all, the federal government is officially $20 trillion in debt and counting. At the same time, technology is advancing at an exponential rate. So it may not be as farfetched as it sounds…

Justin: Doug, what do you make of Atkinson's theory? Could robots really dig us out of this giant hole? And by "us," I mean the federal government, of course.

Doug: Yes, as Tonto said to the Lone Ranger when they were surrounded by hostile Indians: Who is "we"? That's the first key to the answer. I don't see the federal government's debt as being my problem. It's not my debt. I didn't contract for it, and I don't approve of it. I take no personal responsibility for the debt that they've run up. You have to understand that the US Government is a discrete entity, with its own life and interests. It's improper to conflate the government—essentially a million or so creatures that live within the Washington Beltway—with America.

The fact that entrepreneurs develop fantastic technologies, like robots, that increase the amount of real wealth in the world tremendously, shouldn't be seen as a solution to the government's problem. The government debt problem can't be solved with more income. It doesn't matter how many trillions you give them; they'll spend even more. It's the nature of the beast. The only solution is to cut their spending radically, not increase their income radically. Atkinson has the problem upside down.

Justin: Not to mention, the actual federal debt is closer to $200 trillion when you count Social Security, Medicare, and Medicaid. So, there seems to be a lot of wishful thinking baked into this theory.

Doug: Even if increasing government income could pay off the debt, I wouldn't do it. Why not? Because their spending is almost all counterproductive and destructive. They'd have more resources to lavish on the "defense" and "national security" establishments, which act to foment wars abroad and destroy freedom domestically. They'd have more for welfare, which acts to destroy personal responsibility and cement the lower classes to the bottom of society. They'd have more for "education," which at this point is just indoctrination. Most of the money would just find its way into the coffers of the politically connected, so the unjustly rich would just get richer. Almost everything they do does more harm than good. Even if the immediate and direct effects of their actions look good, the delayed and indirect effects are usually disastrous.

So, even if the idea of robotics generating more income for the government worked, it would simply make the problem worse. It's a stupid suggestion.

And it's not just robotics, but any magic technology. Even if friendly aliens landed on the roof of the White House and gave the government a cornucopia, they'd find some way to turn it into a nightmare. You've got to understand that government, and the people who work for it, are more interested in controlling people than controlling things. The problem is everybody's thinking in terms of the government and the government's problems. I'd rather solve problems that, say, Amazon, or Apple, or WalMart have. Those groups provide things that I want, and they don't coerce or tax me like the government. People have to change their whole way of thinking about this.

Because the government, you've got to remember, has a life of its own. The problem is that it doesn't survive by producing. It survives by taking things from its subjects.

Atkinson is right about robots, however. As they become common, they're going to greatly increase the amount of real wealth in the world. Because they have huge advantages, and none of the problems of human workers. If you can be replaced by a robot, then you're already doing inhuman work—dog work. The robot is doing you a favor by taking your brainless job.

Years ago, IBM coined a motto. I don't know if they still use it, but it was great: "Machines should work; people should think." Robots are going to give genuine reality to that meme.

The robot revolution—combined with artificial intelligence, nanotech, genetic engineering, space exploration, and lots of other new fields—are creating an immense amount of wealth. The next question is going to be, well, shouldn't everybody have a guaranteed income? And of course these same people are going to advocate it. My answer to that is no. But let's talk about that another time.

Justin: Yeah, Atkinson misses the mark here wide-left...

The more money you give the State, the more wasteful it becomes. So, the debt wouldn't disappear. It would only get bigger.

Doug: Worse than that, if the government accesses all the new wealth, they're going to wind up using it against you, not for you. Because—let me repeat this for emphasis—the people that gravitate to government are people that are interested not so much in controlling physical reality as they are controlling other people. The problem is the institution itself, not just the temporary party controlling it. So I can't see any good coming from giving more resources to the State.

The question should be: How do we keep that extra wealth out of the government's hands? Not how to put more of it *into* the government's hands. Which seems to be the way these people are thinking.

Justin: If only more people thought that way... Anyway, that's all I've got for today. Thank you for your time, Doug.

Doug: Sure, Justin. Anytime.

Doug Casey on the Modern Space Race

ORIGINALLY PUBLISHED ON MAY 26, 2017

Justin's note: Jeff Bezos is selling nearly $1 billion worth of Amazon stock. Bezos, who founded Amazon, isn't doing this because he's short on cash (he's worth more than $80 billion)... or bearish on Amazon's share price. He's doing this to fund his aerospace company, Blue Origin. As if that weren't crazy enough, Bezos plans to put about $1 billion of his money into Blue Origin every year until the company can sustain itself. Bezos isn't the only billionaire who's set their sights on space, either. Tesla founder Elon Musk has his own aerospace company called SpaceX. In short, a modern space race has broken out between two of the world's richest men...

Justin: Doug, what do you think of this modern-day space race? Are you happy to see billionaires spearheading it instead of governments?

Doug: Absolutely. I don't know if I'd support Bezos' political views—he appears to be more or less in the Soros camp—but the guy's obviously a business genius. He and Musk and others that are getting into the space race are absolutely doing the right thing. Certainly from an intellectual and psychological standpoint. But also from a purely economic one. It's true that pioneers are the ones who might get arrows in their backs. But the risk/reward ratio here is at least as good as it was when Europeans struck out for the New World 500 years ago.

Space is where the future lies from just about every point of view. And I'd much, much rather have private entrepreneurs like them doing this than having NASA do it. Why? Because NASA is a bureaucracy. It doesn't react to profit and loss. They don't either know or care whether they're creating capital or destroying capital.

A bureaucracy follows rules and regulations in an attempt to fulfill the mission. Bureaucracies are necessarily robotic. They're necessarily rigid, unresponsive, and not just non-innovative, but anti innovative. They're all structured like, and act like, the

Post Office or your local DMV. It doesn't matter if the bureaucracy is full of high IQ people, as NASA surely is. The institution itself tends to act stupidly. That's because there are never real incentives for doing a great job, or penalties for a bad job.

That's largely because "cost" and "profit" are alien concepts to bureaucracies. They aren't elements in its decision making. Bureaucracies aren't economic, they're political in the way they calculate their success. But cost and profit are critically important for effectiveness. Something can only be "sustainable"—a very popular buzzword today—if it's profitable. Profit is evidence that you're creating more capital than you're consuming. It's paradoxical that the types who say they're most concerned about sustainability seem most antiprofit in outlook.

Business is going to be much better than NASA ever was in conquering space, for about every reason possible.

It's got to be said that, in its early days, when it was an adventure, NASA wasn't the bureaucracy that it's evolved into today. The concrete hadn't set. But the nature of bureaucracy is such that, as I said, it's built to follow rules, not to create new capital, or innovate. And if something's going to be sustainable, it has to create new capital. It has to produce more wealth than it consumes. So, business is the way that space is going to be conquered, not government.

Justin: I completely agree. It seems conquering people is about the only thing governments do well.

Doug: The State is a coercive entity by its very nature. As Randolph Bourne said 100 years ago, war is the health of the State. So inevitably, they're going to look for military applications of anything that happens with space. And the military applications of space are going to be devastating, potentially much worse than ICBMs with nuclear warheads. It's a question of controlling the high ground. If you're in space and want to launch an attack on another entity, you don't need nuclear weapons. All you need is rocks, which are readily available on the moon or in the asteroid belt, to be dropped down on a country. That can be far more devastating, as the dinosaurs learned.

On a more mundane level, the world increasingly relies on satellites for all kinds of communications. All the major governments are poised to destroy each other's satellites. But, in the meantime, they use most of their own satellites for spying.

So space should be kept out of the hands of governments for just that reason, not to mention the others.

What can be done in space? There are literally no limits. Infinite power from the sun. Infinite materials from the solar system. Zero gravity. No environmental concerns. The possibility exists to do absolutely anything, without the political and social constraints that burden us more than physical factors in many cases. Earth has become a very small place, thanks to technology. So we need technology to increase the human bailiwick. I wish Bezos, Musk and all the other budding space entrepreneurs well. I hope they succeed. And I'm sure they will, in fact, succeed.

Justin: I hope they succeed too, especially since so much seems to be at stake.

In fact, Musk himself has said interplanetary travel is necessary to ensure the continued existence of humanity. Do you think that's true?

Doug: Yeah, absolutely.

It's risky being on just one little ball of dirt in an obscure solar system in one of probably billions of galaxies, each of which contains billions of stars. Most of the stars, it's turning out, have their own planets. It's kind of a new territorial imperative to do this as a species. In a way we're at the same stage the first humans were when they ventured out of Africa 100,000 years ago.

Right now the human race has all its genetic eggs in one basket. Which isn't very smart. Although, looking at this from a philosophical point of view, I'm not sure how much difference it makes to you or me as individuals. And this gets us into the question of what happens after you die. It's not something most people think is relevant to the subject of space migration—but it might be. Space migration is likely indispensable to the continued survival of the species. But how important is that really, on either a personal or a cosmic level?

There seem to be perhaps three logical possibilities. Let me hasten to say I don't have a dog in this fight. I'm simply trying to anticipate some of the consequences of space technology.

One is that you disappear totally when you die. At which point absolutely nothing makes any difference to you. Many people, especially in advanced countries that have cultures of science, hold this view. I'll hazard a wild guess this group is only about 10% of the world population.

A second view. Others, prominently including the Middle Eastern religions that worship Allah, Jesus and Yahweh, think you go to Heaven or Hell. Maybe they're about 40% of world population. I expect they'll suffer an ever-increasing existential crisis as mankind advances further into space, and technologies of all kinds develop.

A third group, including Buddhists and Hindus, believe you're a spiritual entity that's reincarnated. And the only way that it makes any difference what the species does, I think, is if they're right. Only if you're reincarnated do you have a genuine personal interest in what happens to the human race. Of course there are a myriad of theological speculations out there. For all I know, the largest part of humanity doesn't even consider the problem. Be that as it may, the question has big philosophical implications, whether we go into space and get off the planet or not.

Justin: I've never thought about it like that. But that's definitely something to contemplate.

I also have to ask, since you're a betting man… Who do you like in this race: Musk or Bezos?

Doug: I really don't know who's going to win, because you've got to remember that in the aviation race, although Orville and Wilbur Wright were the first ones to fly, they never set up a truly successful aviation company that made planes. I don't know who I'd bet on. And you know Warren Buffett's famous saying about the best thing that could have happened for investors in the airline industry was that someone should have shot the Wrights down. It may be nobody makes money in space for decades…

But I've got to say, I really like Musk's approach. And I love this quotation from him: "I hope to die on Mars, just not on impact." I hope he succeeds in that goal.

Of course, huge advances are being made in life extension too. It's quite likely that somebody that's now alive is going to live for hundreds of years. Which means it's likely many people alive at the turn of the 21st century will see space evolve, the way people alive at the turn of the 20th century saw aviation go from the Wright Brothers to a moon landing. The best part is that there are a half dozen important technologies that are advancing at the rate of Moore's Law. I did an article on them all in the June 2016 issue of *The Casey Report*. [Editor's note: Readers can read that essay here[1] and here[2].] Timothy Leary will turn out to have been conservative in his optimism about what he called SMIILE—Space Migration, Intelligence Increase, Life Extension.

There are all kinds of possibilities that tie into the space race.

Justin: Absolutely. I can only imagine what Musk and Bezos will be working on 20 years from now.

Anyway, that's all I got for today, Doug. Thank you for taking the time to speak with me.

Doug: You're welcome.

Doug Casey on the Militarization of U.S. Police Departments

ORIGINALLY PUBLISHED ON MAY 11, 2017

Justin's note: U.S. police departments are getting more militarized by the day. Here's Doug with more on this disturbing trend…

Justin: Doug, you recently called out anti-drug lawmakers, or what you called "drug warriors," for their immense hypocrisy and stupidity. But what about the growing number of "warrior cops" who seem to view the United States as their own personal battleground?

Doug: I started writing about the militarization of American police back in the 1990s, when it started happening in earnest. And it's very disturbing, because the way a solider deals with the enemy is necessarily quite different from the way the police are supposed to deal with citizens.

The US has these numerous continuing wars around the world, so they wind up with lots of spare military equipment. And what to do with it? They bring it home and give it to the police because they think it might be helpful. And then, driving APCs and wearing body armor, the police get the wrong idea.

Furthermore, all the military vets—many of whom have extra y chromosomes, as do most police generally—like the idea of wearing a uniform and like the idea of carrying a gun and giving and taking orders. They're preferred hires for police forces. But they shouldn't be, because you inevitably pick up bad habits, and inappropriate skills, hanging out in a war zone.

All these things compound upon the other. It's a very bad trend. I see no reason why that trend is going to turn around. In fact, I expect it to accelerate, especially as the economy turns downhill and people become more restless and the Deep State feels that the plebs have to be kept under control. So, yeah, it's a trend that's been accelerating for several decades. And it's going to keep accelerating until some type of a crisis blows it all up.

Justin: Yeah, I can only imagine how much US police departments will up the ante when the next financial crisis arrives.

Doug: That's right.

Another key distinction here is that there are two ways police can relate to society. One is as peacekeepers, and the other is as law enforcers. Keeping the peace just makes sure that the bad elements of society don't become violent or don't violate other people's rights to life and property—that's basically it. That's what a peace officer does. Other than that, he keeps his nose out of everybody's business.

But the people in today's police aren't brought up to think that way. They're indoctrinated to think in terms of law enforcement—totally different thing. Because there are thousands and thousands and thousands of laws—federal, state, local—and they're supposed to enforce them all; it has nothing to do with keeping the peace. This is another bad trend which is bound to accelerate.

Justin: It's scary to think how much more militarized US police departments could become. They already have grenade launchers and armored personnel carriers, after all. And now, the state of Connecticut wants to give its police officers drones that fire missiles. What could they possibly want next?

Doug: Yeah, what could possibly go wrong? It's one reason why I'm actually quite happy to be living kind of off the grid in a rather remote place in Argentina. These things aren't even being imagined, much less happening, down here. It really seems like every trend, every single trend in the US, is going the wrong way. It's completely out of control.

Where will it end? Science fiction has always been a much, much better predictor of the future than any think tank. A couple of movies come to mind. One is *Running Man*, 1987, now 30 years ago, with Arnold Schwarzenegger. In it, Arnold plays a cop righteously hunting down accused miscreants, for the amusement of the hoi polloi. Their trial and punishment was basically a game show. It anticipates the direction of today's shows like *Cops* and *Bad Boys*. These shows always make the cops out as upstanding heroes. The offenders are generally lower-middle-class whites, for drug violations, and not blacks—that would be too politically incorrect.

In *Total Recall*, 1990, they deal with the subject of pre-crime—predicting who is likely to commit what felony, and taking preemptive action. In fact, neuroscientists are making great strides to determine pre-crime. Very disturbing—you'd better look, act, and think like a good little lamb to avoid being locked up.

And then, of course, Orwell's *1984* and Aldous Huxley's *Brave New World*. Things are evolving in the direction of both books, simultaneously.

Justin: Thanks for sharing your thoughts, Doug.

Doug: My pleasure.

Doug Casey on the Opioid Crisis

ORIGINALLY PUBLISHED ON MAY 10, 2017

Justin's note: "Enjoy looking over your shoulder, constantly wondering if today's the day we come for you. Enjoy trying to sleep tonight, wondering if tonight's the night our SWAT team blows your front door off the hinges. We are coming for you." This sounds like something from an '80s action movie. But that's an actual quote from the Lake County Sheriff's Office in Tavares, Florida. Sheriff Grinnell delivered this message last month while flanked by four combat-ready officers wearing ski masks. Grinnell's message was aimed at local drug dealers. You see, Lake County has a serious opioid problem. And like many other places in the US, it's fighting its drug problem as if it were a war…

Justin: Doug, what do you make of the opioid crisis?

Doug: The news cycle seems to be emphasizing the use of opioids at the moment. Now, these are almost all legal prescription drugs, not illegally smuggled heroin and morphine, as was the case in *The French Connection*. People get their doctors to prescribe opioids for pain. Of course, pain is not something that you can prove. So it's legitimate for doctors to prescribe these things. After a while the patient may develop a chemical dependency.

This gets into why people become addicted. I'm of the opinion that all kinds of addictions, not just the opioids in question, but addictions to cocaine, meth, other kinds of narcotics, alcohol, or anything else are basically because of pain.

But it's not necessarily physical pain. It's psychological pain, which may be even more important. And psychological pain means that people want to check out of reality. So as the economy gets worse—and I think it will get much, much worse in the near future—you can expect levels of addiction to skyrocket, not to go down.

Addiction is a bad habit, but it's nobody else's business. From an ethical point of view, your primary possession is your own body. If you don't own it, and have a right to do whatever you want with it, then you in fact have no rights at all. That's why the drug war itself is criminal, and morally insane.

The efforts of dangerous idiots like Sheriff Grinnell are counterproductive. If they confiscate a ton of drugs, that just drives up the market price for those that remain. And increases the profits of dealers, drawing more dealers into the business. And encouraging addicts who can't afford the higher prices to turn to crime in order to support their habit. That's entirely apart from increasing the level of violence in society, corrupting the police, and lots of other negative fallout.

I'm always amazed by the immense hypocrisy and stupidity of the drug warriors, as well.

For instance, Rush Limbaugh has always been a major drug warrior. He's actually said on his show that junkies should be executed because they're such a danger. And then, what do you know? Turns out that he was an oxycodone junkie. Just like the major crusaders against homosexuality—*mirabile dictu*—turn out to be closet queers themselves half the time. Like Larry Craig, the Republican Senator who claimed he just had a "wide stance" in a public men's room.

These people seem driven to make laws against the very things they most fear in themselves.

Justin: What's fueling this crisis?

Doug: Well, many of these opioids are being paid for by Medicaid and Medicare. So the government's actually paying for the drug boom.

And it's especially perverse because drugs were a non-problem before the Harrison Act, which was passed in 1914. The act basically made all opium and coca derivatives illegal in the US. Before that there were very few people that were addicted to narcotics, even though narcotics were available to anybody at the local corner drugstore. Addicts were looked down on as suffering from a moral failure, but there was no more profit in heroin than in aspirin. So there were no cartels or drug gangs.

What we're dealing with isn't a medical problem, it's a psychological, even a spiritual, problem. And a legal problem, because self-righteous busybodies keep passing laws—with very severe penalties—regulating what people can or can't do with their own bodies. It's part of the general degradation of civilization that I've been putting my finger on over the last few years.

The government is the problem behind addiction, on all levels. It's a major cause for people feeling psychological pain. And they're the sole reason these medicines are illegal and unavailable. On the subject of addiction, people can become addicted to most anything—food, sugar, alcohol, gambling, sleep, sex—you name it. It's not good when you do too much of absolutely anything. But so what?

Justin: So, I take it prohibition isn't the answer?

Doug: Illegalizing something does nothing but create a black market and give people a reason to induce other people to get high. I mean, people have been drinking alcohol for about the last 10,000 years. But it didn't become a real problem until the Eighteenth Amendment and the Volstead Act passed in 1920. At that point, it financed the mafia. Laws turn simple bad habits into massive and profitable criminal enterprises.

The government learned absolutely nothing from the failure of alcohol prohibition. What they're doing with drugs makes an occasional, trivial problem into a national catastrophe...

Justin: Thanks for sharing your thoughts, Doug.

Doug: My pleasure.

Doug Casey on Why It's OK to Discriminate

ORIGINALLY PUBLISHED ON APRIL 25, 2017

Justin's note: It was the worst article I've ever read. The piece was titled "Could It Be Time To Deny White Men The Franchise?" In it, the author argued why white men should no longer be allowed to vote. As soon as I finished reading the article, I sent it to Doug…

Justin: Doug what did you think of that *Huffington Post* article I sent you?

Doug: I read the article when it was still up, and it was absolutely incredible. That's not just a figure of speech. I mean it beggared belief. I urge everyone reading this to hit the link[1]. These people don't seem to realize that they're actually parodies of themselves. I mean, they're always talking about racism and xenophobia and sexism and ageism and the like. They don't look at people as individuals, they look at people as members of classes. That's why it's called "identity politics"—you don't identify as an individual, but as a member of a group or a class. And, of course, their philosophical background is cultural Marxism. Because, you know, one of the central points of Marxism is that people are all members of classes.

But it's actually gone beyond that. It's become fashionable now to hate white males in particular. They say that women, blacks, Muslims—pick a group, any group except for white males—are all discriminated against.

I would say, in the first place, there's absolutely nothing wrong with discrimination in itself. Discrimination can be rational. Discrimination can be intelligent. It's often necessary. It's a matter of what you're basing your discrimination on.

---

1. www.huffingtonpost.co.za/shelley-garland/could-it-be-time-to-deny-white-men-the-franchise_a_22036640/

You have to discriminate between things that will help you and things that will hurt you. And that can include other groups or even other people. It's a genetic trait to be more favorably inclined towards people like yourself. Tribes usually identify themselves as "the people", and everybody else is "other", a potential enemy. It makes sense to recognize facts of reality. Different ethnic and religious groups have different beliefs, customs, and ethics. Until you can get to know them as individuals it makes sense to generalize.

But it goes deeper than that with this insane article. What these people really hate is Western Civilization and everything it represents. The question is: Why do these people think it's virtuous to discriminate against white males? White males are largely responsible for Western Civilization. Which is shorthand for things like individualism, free markets, free thought, science, literature, industry, and about everything that's allowed mankind to rise out of the muck and look to conquer the planets.

That's what this article really hates.

So, it's fascinating not so much that somebody wrote an article as stupid as that. But that a large outlet like *Huffington* would actually publish it. It's a sign of how degraded things are. I'd say the author suffers from a serious psychological aberration. The editor who posted it is clearly a graduate of some PC US university, probably a major in Gender Studies.

It's too bad that they took it down because it should be put on display, as a warning. Unless they repost it in *The Onion*.

Justin: I totally agree, Doug. I've also noticed that these people don't really want equality for all. They want equality for some. It's incredibly hypocritical.

Doug: It's actually all about envy. Envy is a vice—it's different from jealousy, another vice. Jealousy is a vice that says, "You have something, I want it, I'll take it away from you." Envy is even worse. It says, "You have something that I want, I can't get it, so I'll destroy it, so you can't have it either." These people aren't just misguided. They're mentally ill. They're actually evil. But they're not just taken seriously, they're treated with respect. And they're endemic to society at this point. This is cause for great pessimism.

Justin: It's certainly not the only reason to be pessimistic, either. But that's it for today. Thank you for taking the time to speak with me.

Doug: You're welcome.

Doug Casey on Trump's Attack on Syria

ORIGINALLY PUBLISHED ON APRIL 12, 2017

Justin's note: In April 2017, the US military launched 59 Tomahawk missiles at Syria as retaliation for a chemical attack that killed at least 70 people, including children. Some people think this barbaric attack absolutely warrants retaliation. Other people, like myself, think the US government should mind its own business, since these affairs often turn into costly, never-ending conflicts. That said, this is a highly complex situation. I don't claim to have all the answers. But if there's anyone who understands this situation, it's Doug…

Justin: Doug, the US just launched a major attack on Syria.

Are you surprised Trump did this? Keep in mind, he publicly criticized Obama for wanting to attack Syria in 2013. He also said that the President should get approval from Congress before attacking Syria. He didn't do that, either.

Doug: I'm actually not too surprised. The problem with Trump is that he doesn't have any core philosophical beliefs. He apparently has no idea what's right or wrong, good or bad, other than the way he feels. And what he feels doesn't reflect a well thought out worldview, but just his background or the way he's been brought up. Like most people, he's a creature of his emotions, not his intellect. So, he's capable of doing absolutely anything on the spur of the moment.

Now, I supported Trump because he wasn't Hillary. The fact that he said he wanted to "drain the swamp" told me that he wanted to change the ways of Washington. But it appears that his idea is simply to make Washington more efficient, which is a mistake. He has no clue that the essence of government is coercion—or maybe he does, which would be even worse. When you have institutionalized coercion, the last thing you want to do is make it more efficient.

But one thing is certain: he won't succeed in making government "better." Sure, he wants to decrease the amount of regulation from dysfunctional agencies like the EPA. But he's just going to trim them. He doesn't see any principles involved. Trimming these destructive agencies is like pruning a plant: it just allows them to grow back even stronger. They have to be pulled out by the roots, and the ground they grow in should be salted. Or sprayed with Roundup. Or maybe flooded with Agent Orange.

As for his foreign policy, the fact that he says we're going to "destroy ISIS" is idiocy. ISIS has never done anything to the US. None of those countries over there have. Of course ISIS is nasty. But it's not our problem. It's the problem of people in the region. In fact, as a regime, ISIS is just as legitimate as any other over there. Including our loyal "allies" the Saudis. At this point, most everybody in the region has learned to hate, disrespect, and distrust the US. The US has won the Trifecta for stupidity.

And now he's attacking the Assad regime, which has done nothing against the US. Sure, that regime had secret police, and has done some unpleasant things. But they all do, including all our "friends"—which once prominently included Saddam Hussein. In fact the Assad regime was and is quite mellow; the man is a Western-educated doctor. If you're going to hold together a completely artificial country with about a score of mutually antagonistic groups, that's what has to be done. Incidentally, trying to hold it all together is really stupid, but that's another subject…

Regarding those guys in the gym, I promise you none of them can even find Syria on the map. All they think they know is what they've heard in the popular media, and the media itself just repeats things they hear. Most of it from highly suspect sources.

Did the Assad government launch a gas attack? Highly unlikely. They're not that stupid; they realize that using gas in a real no-no in today's world. Even Churchill, who advocated using gas against the Mesopotamian natives after WW1, wouldn't dream of it today. It would just give a foreign government—like the US—the excuse they need to attack.

Further, from a purely military point of view, gas makes no sense. In today's world there are much more precise and effective ways to get the job done. Especially considering the detailed reporting—what reporters would go into that war zone today?—the whole thing seems fabricated.

But the gym guys like this kind of macho nonsense. They like the idea of "decisive action," "showing toughness," and "doing something." If they thought that the children they're supposed to be so concerned about were Muslims who might grow up to be Jihadis, they might be less outraged.

Justin: Will this attack on Syria accomplish anything? Is this even a winnable battle?

Doug: It will accomplish nothing except to antagonize a bunch of people whose family and friends get killed. I mean the cost of each of those missiles—the hard cost is about $1 million plus ancillary costs. Where does Trump think that money is coming from? Does he think the Chinese are going to lend us even more to do that type of thing?

It's actually quite comical, at least if you have a sense of black humor. Trump may see it as boosting US exports to the tunc of $59 million of missiles. And simultaneously helping a friend somewhere among the approximately 2,341 armed groups over there that hate the US government.

The attack was economically idiotic in the here and now. It's at once destroying capital over there, and adding to debt in the US. The world was made poorer. It's not making any friends; it's making more enemies. It's alienating a lot of people in the US who hoped he would disinvolve the US from foreign adventures. After this, you have to take his bellicose rhetoric against ISIS, North Korea, and everybody else, seriously.

The attack served no useful purpose whatsoever. Except to get neocons to say he was acting "presidential."[1] Trump appears to have no idea even who's kind of a friend and who's definitely an enemy of either him or the US.

And at this point, the US has no friends over there. It just has people who are different degrees of enemy. The attack shows zero useful purpose—zero. Any

---

1. www.cnn.com/videos/politics/2017/04/07/fareed-zakaria-trump-became-president-syria-newday.cnn

thoughtful person has to say "Wow. This guy could really get completely out of control." It's idiocy. And scary.

Justin: Speaking of antagonizing other countries, Russia called the US attack on Syria an "act of aggression." It also said the strikes "struck a significant blow to Russian-American relations, which were already in a sorry state."

Do you think tensions between the US and Russia will escalate because of this attack?

Doug: There's no question about that. You know, one of the things I liked about Trump was that he seemed to want a détente, to even be friendly, with the Russians. Which would be smart. I think the Russians will go out of their way to avoid a war—their government is much more intelligent than ours—but accidents can happen. These things can spin out of control just as easily as they did a hundred years ago at the start of World War I. One things leads to another, and it becomes unpredictable.

I'm not just afraid that Trump may open Pandora's Box in the Middle East. He might do the same on the border with Russia in the Baltics or in the Ukraine.

Even worse than that, the Chinese think that the South and East China seas are their territories, much in the same way that the US thinks all the seas next to the US are its territories. And it's very provocative having carrier groups floating around there, basically looking for trouble. Which will be easy to find because of US alliances with the South Koreans, the Taiwanese, the Filipinos, and the Japanese, among others. It would be the same if the Chinese sent their Navy off the coast of Santa Catalina. It would be considered very provocative.

So, it's likely to end badly.

Justin: It's certainly unsettling. Yet, US stocks hung in there on Friday. They actually closed the day slightly up. This tells me investors aren't taking this situation seriously.

More importantly, it doesn't seem like anything can shake the confidence of investors at this point. What do you make of this?

Doug: Well, a trend in motion tends to stay in motion until a crisis hits. So, it's very hard to call a top to the stock market.

I mean I've been saying for a long time that the market's overpriced. But there's no telling how much more overpriced it can get. I don't want to pick a top.

But I will say this. In the stock market, the way you make money is by buying when things appear to be cheap and people are afraid. And right now, things don't look cheap and people aren't afraid. I don't see why anyone wants to own stocks. In fact, I'm starting to buy out of the money puts on the S&P.

The problem is that, while it seems metaphysically impossible for everything to be overpriced, everything is overpriced, with the exception of commodities. They're actually cheap. Most miners and farmers are losing money at current metal and agricultural prices. But it's a very, very tough environment. The name of the game over the next few years is just keeping what you have.

Justin: Yeah, I guess we'll have to wait and see what happens. Maybe if tensions between the US and Russia flare up, that could be what finally puts this bull market in US stocks to rest.

Doug: It's quite a problem because stocks are in a bubble. Bonds are in a super bubble. Real estate is in a bubble.

It's hard to buy commodities because they might still go lower—but I'm friendly towards them, even though commodities have been in a bear market, in real terms, for the last 10,000 years. Cash is dangerous because banks are all bankrupt and the dollar is losing value. So, it's a very unusual economic time.

The smartest thing to do is own cash, gold, and silver. You can speculate on little mining stocks, as a leverage play on gold of course. But it's very tough—much tougher than during the '70s and '80s. Which, I'm aware, seems like ancient history to many.

But let me conclude by saying that the problems we have in the markets are going to be completely trivial if we get into a really serious war. Not just the kind of sport wars that have been popular since Vietnam, but a serious war. And that's possible.

Justin: Let's hope it doesn't come to that. Anyway, thank you for sharing your thoughts, Doug.

Doug: My pleasure.

Doug Casey on the Coming Holy War

ORIGINALLY PUBLISHED ON APRIL 6, 2017

Justin's note: Turkey's foreign minister recently said that "wars of religion" are coming to Europe. This is a major warning sign…

Justin: Doug, Turkey's foreign minister recently said that "wars of religion" are coming to Europe. Do you think this could actually happen?

Doug: Well, human nature hasn't changed in many thousands of years. And religion is important to the human animal. Perhaps it's always been something that people were prone to fight about, but the historical record shows that religious wars only started with the invention of Judaism, Christianity and Islam. Of course, these religions—which have always been at war with each other, and all other religions—are similar in that they believe in one god. Pagan religions were and are accepting of other people's gods and beliefs.

The question is, which god is the right one? Should you believe in Yahweh, or Jesus, or Allah? Because it appears to me that they're all very different, based upon what they say and what they have their followers believe. Islam and Christianity have been duking it out since the 7th century, and that's unlikely to change. They both claim to have the one and only true god, but they're very different gods—not at all the same one. So it's an irreconcilable difference.

Justin: So, the ingredients for a holy war have always been there?

Doug: Yes. Up to about 100 years ago, Christians felt a moral obligation to convert everyone, including other misguided Christians. Now it's mostly just the Muslims who feel that way. It's entirely possible, even likely, we're going to have an outright war of religion. Although, in the highly Politically Correct West, it will have to be called something else.

The ongoing invasion of Europe by Muslims is one aspect of it—although that's not so much a religious thing *per se*. That's partly because the Muslims are migrating mostly for economic reasons. And because religion is a dead duck in Europe today. Europe is a post-Christian society. Very few people go to church or take Christianity seriously in Europe, it's a very secular society. Which is a bit of a problem, because they've taken the State for their new god.

But the State doesn't promise anybody an afterlife. So, in my opinion, Europeans are actually ripe for conversion to Islam. It's a serious problem, because Islam is incompatible with, and antithetical to Western Civilization.

Justin: Why should the average American care about this?

Doug: It's part of the gradual destruction of Western culture. Lots of termites—including socialism, cultural Marxism, gender warfare—have been eating away at the foundations of Western Civilization for decades. Islam, in itself, isn't a real threat. The Koran, which PC types love to treat with respect, is just poorly written medieval sci-fi. It's living proof that humans are capable of believing absolutely anything.

That said, Islam is a threat to the West because tens of millions of migrants are being invited to come and live at the expense of the current residents. Europe will collapse from within, as did Rome. The average European believes in nothing—except that his civilization not only isn't worthy, but is actually evil. No wonder the migrants treat them with contempt.

The Mohammedans—although I'll note it's now very un-PC to call them that—are technologically and economically backward. As long as they put the Koran at the center of their lives—and they have to, because it is the direct, incontrovertible word of Allah—they'll remain backward. If, through an accident of geology, there wasn't a lot of low cost oil in places they live, the West would have no reason to care what they think, say, or do. They'd be no more than an interesting tourist attraction.

The good news is that, over the next 100 years, most Muslims will fall away from their primitive beliefs. But that's another story… And a lot is going to happen in the meantime.

Justin: Doug, I know you think the European Union (EU) has been destined to fail from the start. Could religious tensions spark this inevitable crisis? Or will an economic or financial crisis be the final nail in the EU's coffin?

Doug: Religion is definitely playing into the crisis. Because you have to remember that, in continental Europe, Kosovo, Albania, and Turkey, are already Muslim, as are parts of Bulgaria. 10% of Western Europe is already Muslim. There are about 20 million Muslims in southern Russia, and that's going to be a big problem for Moscow. There's always blowback from running an empire, something the French and British have found as well. And Americans are discovering. Enemy sympathizers are already within the gates. London is turning into Karachi, Paris into Kinshasa, and Rome into Lagos.

I wouldn't doubt that there's going to be a war against Islam. Even though, as I said, very few Europeans take Christianity seriously anymore. Islam, however, is much more virulent than Christianity—it's like Christianity in the Middle Ages. Even if the average Muslim is basically "get along go along" with his religion in daily life, when push comes to shove, yeah, he takes his religion quite seriously—the way Christians did hundreds of years ago. So this is very serious.

It's a cultural war, much more than an economic or military one. And I'm afraid the West has already about lost it. It's really tragic, because almost everything good in the world has come out of the West—in particular freedom, capitalism, individualism, science, technology, literature. Future generations will miss them. It's sad.

Justin: Doug, thank you for sharing your thoughts with us.

Doug: Sure, anytime.

Doug Casey on Why College Is a Waste of Money

ORIGINALLY PUBLISHED ON APRIL 3, 2017

Justin's note: The cost of a college education is getting out of hand. Here's Doug with his insights on this troubling trend…

Justin: Doug, I recently had an interesting conversation with my sister.

She told me that her financial advisor suggested she start setting aside $500 to $1,000 a month to pay for her son's college education. That's because a four-year college education is apparently going to cost between $400,000 and $500,000 18 years from now.

Her advisor clearly arrived at this figure based on how fast college tuition costs have been rising, which is about 6% per year based on my research.

But you have to wonder if the cost can keep rising at this rate. It seems to me that no one will go to college if it's going to cost a half-million bucks.

What do you make of this trend?

Doug: Well, the first thing—my advice to your sister is to get a new financial advisor. I fear that she's relying on a complete imbecile. She should fire him immediately, and for a number of reasons.

Number one is his assumption that the trend of higher college costs is going to continue to a totally unaffordable level. In fact, the cost/benefit ratio of going to college is already so out of whack that the whole system has to change radically. A college degree, even now, is of only marginal value; most everybody has one. And things that everybody has are devalued. You're quite correct that colleges and universities today are dead ducks as businesses. Unless you're going to learn a trade, like doctoring or lawyering, or you're going for science, engineering, or math, where you need the formal discipline and where you need lab courses, it's a total misallocation, even a waste of money to go to college today.

So I applaud the fact that all these colleges and universities are dead men walking, that they're all going to go bankrupt. They are totally overrun and infested with cultural Marxists and progressives, militant leftists that are propagandizing kids with absolutely the wrong kind of values. It's astonishing that parents are willing to pay even today's prices to subject their kids to four years of indoctrination. So I'm glad that they're all going bankrupt.

Justin: But don't you need a college education to get ahead in life?

Doug: It's not necessary to go to college. You're likely to be corrupted, and in-debt yourself like an indentured servant for many years to come. The question is: Do you want an education, or do you just want a piece of paper that says you logged the time in a classroom? These are two different things. Getting an education is strictly a matter of motivation and self-discipline, not paying money to sit in a classroom. If you've got half a brain, you realize that you want the knowledge, not the diploma, and there's no necessary correlation between them. Nobody can "give" you an education; it's something you must gain for yourself.

Most top universities now have their courses online. You can get an education by listening to these courses. And even when you're driving your car, you should be playing CDs by The Teaching Company. They have the best professors in the world giving command performance lectures. And you can hear them an unlimited number of times. This is much better than listening to some also-ran drone on, while you may have cut the class, or be half asleep, or not taking good notes.

Technology has changed the whole landscape of education. Its cost is approaching zero, not the stratosphere, as your sister's advisor seems to think. If the kids insist on going to college and indenturing themselves, as well as cluttering their minds with irrelevancies and false data, then they should only consider, say, Harvard, or very few schools like it. At least there the prestige, and qualifications for admission, are so high that the connections they make may compensate for the many downsides.

And anyway, Ray Kurzweil's right about the Singularity, in my opinion. And he's upped the date to when it's going to occur to 2029, which is only 12 years from now, at which point the whole world will have changed in ways that will change the nature of life itself. So forget about saving to send your kids to college; and that goes double for your grandkids.

Justin: I thought the same thing, Doug.

You see, my sister's advisor suggested that she and her husband set up a 529 plan, which is basically a tax-friendly way to save money for college. I asked her what would happen to the money if her son didn't go to college. She said she could use the money to pay her for grandchildren's college education.

But, like you said, the world is going to be very different 12 years from now. Who knows what it's going to look like 40 or 50 years from now?

Doug: Over the next generation the world is going to change totally and unrecognizably from the way it is right now. Technological change is compounding at an exponential rate. It's always been exponential, quite frankly. Ever since the invention of fire. But we're now in its later stages; it's like a Saturn rocket taking off, very slowly at first, but constantly accelerating[1].

It's going to be fascinating and fantastic to watch what happens over the next 20 years. And relying on, and paying for, today's educational paradigm makes as much sense as entering a Model T Ford in the 24 Hours of Le Mans.

Justin: I agree 100%. We're living in very exciting times.

Anyway, thank you for taking the time to speak with me, Doug. It was a pleasure, as always.

Doug: You're welcome.

---

1. www.caseyresearch.com/doug-casey-on-the-next-industrial-revolution/

Doug Casey on the Political Correctness Movement

ORIGINALLY PUBLISHED ON MARCH 20, 2017

Justin's note: Doug isn't just a world-class speculator. He's also a rare, independent thinker and a walking encyclopedia of knowledge. Best of all, Doug isn't afraid to speak his mind… Here's what he had to say about political correctness…

Justin: I want to ask you about political correctness (PC). Obviously, PC culture's nothing new, but it kind of seems like it's spreading like cancer these days.

For example, I recently read that the University of Minnesota is dropping the names "Homecoming King and Queen" in favor of "Royals." They're doing this in the name of "gender inclusivity."

Is PC culture getting totally out of hand, or am I going crazy?

Doug: Parts of the culture are borderline insane. There've been news items regarding this on scores of different colleges and universities across the US. What you mention at the University of Minnesota, is just part of a greater movement. Although I've got to say that I find the use of "Royals" objectionable. I dislike the idea of a hereditary aristocracy—kings and queens and royals. They're basically just successful, silk-clad gangsters. Why the royal family in Britain is looked up to is a mystery to me. They, like all royals in the world, historically are just descendants of successful thugs.

But that's not the point that the PC people are making. They don't want to see people identified by their birth sex. They would rather that people "identify" as whatever gender—and I understand there are supposed to be about 40—you feel you belong to. You can say you are whoever you think you are. And oddly enough, I'm somewhat sympathetic to that. I think you should be able to call yourself what you want, do what you want, say what you want, this is all fine. And let people judge you by how you identify yourself. Say that you're a hermaphrodite dinosaur who was born on Mars, if you want. I don't care; it's your problem. But these PC types want to legislate that people have to treat the psychologically aberrated as if they were normal. They want laws and punishments governing what you can and can't do and say and even feel. They want to force you to respect, and pay for, the fantasies of a minority. And change, overturn, actually, the whole social culture of the country. It's a very disturbing trend. It's likely to end in violence.

I believe I first heard the term "political correctness" used on a Saturday Night Live show back in about 1980. And I thought it was just a joke—like most of the things on SNL. But it turned out to be a real thing, and it's been building momentum, for at least the last two generations. Where is it going to end? I'm not sure, but it's just one more termite eating away at the foundations of Western civilization itself. People that go along with this stuff aren't just crazy. They're actually evil. They're the same types who rallied around Robespierre during the French revolution, Lenin during the Russian Revolution, Hitler in '30s Germany, and Mao in China. It's a certain personality type.

The fact that the average American still puts up with this kind of nonsense and treats it with respect is a bad sign. PC values are continually inculcated into kids that go off to college—which, incidentally, is another idiotic mistake that most people make for both economic and philosophical reasons. It's a real cause for pessimism.

Justin: I agree 100%, Doug. But here's something our average reader might not realize.

The PC "movement" is actually happening across the world.

For example, Cardiff Metropolitan University in the U.K. recently banned words like "mankind," "homosexual," "housewife," "manmade," and "sportsmanship" in an effort to "promote fairness and equality through raising awareness about potentially discriminatory vocabulary."

Here are some of the University's approved alternatives…

Instead of "manpower," students and faculty should say "human resources."

Instead of "mankind," "humanity."

Instead of "sportsmanship," "fairness."

Instead of "polio victim," "polio survivor."

So, here we have another university trying to legislate what people can and cannot say in the name of fairness and equality.

But I really don't see how this accomplishes anything. Would you agree?

Justin: Completely. The words you use control the way you think. These people don't have good intentions, they have bad intentions. Destructive intentions. They're opposed to all the things that, starting with Ancient Greece, made Western Civilization unique, and better than any other on Earth. They're opposed to the concepts of individualism, personal freedom, capitalism, economic liberty, free thought, and the like. And it starts with controlling the words you use. George Orwell pointed that out in 1984 where he created "Newspeak," which was a new version of the English language that used all kinds of different new words in order to change the way people think. And to make it impossible for them to think clearly, because the words were purposely misdefined, often to the opposite of the meanings that they actually have. So, sure, this is part of the continuing corruption of Western civilization itself.

And you're right, it's not just in American universities. It's in universities everywhere, because the culture of universities everywhere has been controlled by this whole class of progressives, social justice warriors, cultural Marxists, socialists—they go under a number of names. I don't know what's going to be done about it, quite frankly, because the average person doesn't have A) the backbone and B) the philosophical knowledge to counter these people. So there's great cause for pessimism, watching this happen and accelerate. It's not slowing down, it's accelerating everywhere.

For instance, some years ago I sat on the Board of Trustees of two different universities. The other trustees weren't academics, but normal, successful middle class people. And they were completely snowed by these crazy trends. They were of good will, but they'd been brainwashed by their own educations, and the culture around them, into thinking that although perhaps the SJWs and such were going "too far," they didn't actively oppose them. I'm afraid the intellectual/psychological battle has been lost.

Justin: Exactly, it seems people across the world are waging a war on their own freedom of speech. Meanwhile, you have the government waging a war on people's privacy…

As I'm sure you saw, WikiLeaks recently released a series of documents and files that show the CIA is hacking people's smartphones, computers, and internet-connected televisions.

As disturbing as this news is, I can't say I'm surprised. Were you?

Justin: No, I wasn't at all surprised by it. But people's reaction to these horrible things is that, "Well, the CIA should be reined in a bit, they should be brought under control." But this is the wrong reaction. The CIA—along with the NSA, the DEA, and a bunch of others—should be abolished, because the CIA has become an actual Praetorian guard. It's become a government within a government. They have their own armed forces, they have their own sources of income. You can go rogue within the CIA, and if you're powerful enough or clever enough you can basically do what you want because you're an armed government agent that's a member of a very powerful group.

These people are completely out of control. And they have a powerful propaganda machine that works around the clock to convince ignorant and paranoid Boobus americanus that they're actually good guys, working for his interests against the rest of the world.

The CIA should be abolished because it's dysfunctional, but also because it serves no useful purpose. It's never ever predicted, through its so-called "intelligence gathering," anything of value—ever. The Korean War, the rise of Castro, the fall of the Shah, the rise of Islam, the fact that the Soviet Union was just an empty shell—you know, they thought the Soviet Union was actually competing with the US from an economic point of view. They're always absolutely wrong on everything. It defies the odds of pure chance. They're not just useless, but extremely dangerous. All the coups and revolutions they've plotted were disasters.

Can you abolish them? Can you get rid of them at this point? No, they're far too powerful. And anybody that tries is either going to be killed and/or discredited by their black propaganda. At this point the situation's completely out of control, and we just have to see where it ends. As an individual American, you should try to insulate yourself from these people. Because they're not going away; they're going to become even more powerful.

Justin: How can the average American do that? Should they flee to another country? Is this something people can even escape?

Justin: It's now a very small world, so it's very hard to escape. But you just mentioned something to consider. I spend 2/3rds of the year in South America, and travel a lot. Believe it or not, I don't personally have a cell phone, because I don't like to feel tethered to an electronic device. Societies down here aren't nearly as electronically oriented as they are in the US. Though my Internet connection in Cafayate, Argentina is much better then the one I have in Aspen. So, yes, that's one thing. It's easier to be out of sight and out of mind of the bad guys if you're out of the US, which is the epicenter of all of this. I think that's important. And being physically absent and trying to limit your use of electronic devices and be careful when you do use them. That's about all you can do at this point.

Or you can be a good little lamb, and never think out of the box. To mix metaphors, you can act like an ostrich and stick your head in the sand, believing you have nothing to hide, because you're one of the herd who never does anything wrong. Too few people have read Harvey Silverglate's book where he points out how the average American often commits about three felonies a day.

But that book is surely inaccurate. It's 10 years old. Now it's probably like five felonies a day.